THE
TWO REVOLUTIONS

The
Two Revolutions

An Eye-witness Study of Russia 1917

A BACKGROUND BOOK

R. H. Bruce Lockhart

With a Foreword and Postscript

The Achievements
of the Russian Revolution

by John Keep

DUFOUR EDITIONS

CHESTER SPRINGS

PENNSYLVANIA

Foreword and Postscript © John Keep 1967
Library of Congress Catalog Card number: 67–24887
Manufactured in Great Britain
First published in the U.S.A. 1967

CONTENTS

FOREWORD

Of all the events that have changed the course of modern history, few have been more decisive than the Russian Revolution, which reached its climax just fifty years ago. In March, 1917, the Romanov dynasty, which had ruled Russia for over 300 years, was overthrown. The Emperor Nicholas II abdicated and a democratic liberal Provisional Government came to power. A bare eight months later, after many vicissitudes, this Government was itself overthrown. On the night of November 6–7, 1917, the Bolsheviks, led by Vladimir Ilyich Lenin, seized power in Petrograd, the present Leningrad. A Soviet Government was established which, in forbidding conditions of war and economic breakdown, set about the almost superhuman task of building the world's first socialist state, which we know today as the Union of Soviet Socialist Republics. The roots of the present competition of ideas between East and West go back to this crucial turning point in human affairs.

One of the few living British eye-witnesses of these stirring events was Sir Robert Bruce Lockhart, KCMG, who was then HM Consul-General in Moscow. In 1918 he headed a special diplomatic mission to the new Soviet Government, was arrested by the Bolsheviks, and imprisoned for a time in the Kremlin—an experience which he has described in his best-selling book, *Memoirs of a British Agent*.

In the present volume Sir Robert draws a vivid picture of the Revolution and its antecedents. He conveys the feel of life in Imperial Russia in the halcyon days before the First World War, and traces the course of the revolutionary movement from its nineteenth-century origins to the great crisis of 1917. The Revolution did not fulfil all the hopes entertained by Russian liberals and democrats. Under Communist dictatorship Russia sacrificed her freedom for the sake of economic progress and political aggrandisement. Yet the Soviet regime has many achievements to its credit.

A Postscript reviews developments over the past half-century and places the Revolution in the perspective of today.

JOHN KEEP

London,
December, 1966

Note: Dates are given in New Style, i.e., according to the Gregorian calendar, which was adopted in Russia on February 1/14, 1918. To convert dates to the Julian calendar previously in use, 12 days should be subtracted in the nineteenth century and 13 in the twentieth.

I

The Historical Background

'The inter-action of despotism and freedom, of education and slavery, this is the squaring of the circle—the riddle which we have been solving for two centuries since Peter the Great and which is still unsolved.'—*Vasily Kliuchevsky*.

'Bolshevism is not an episode in Russian history. It is an organic disease of the Russian people.'—*Nicholas Berdiaev*.

I

The Revolutionary Spirit

IT is customary for historians to trace the development of the Russian revolutionary spirit from the French Revolution and from the Russian officers who, returning home after the final defeat of Napoleon, brought back with them the liberal ideas with which they had been infected by the West.

It is a useful date, but it ignores the destructive element in the Russian character which, like the Russian climate, swings rapidly from one extreme to the other. There is no kinder, gentler, more superstitiously religious people than the Russian people; no people readier in their strength to sacrifice their lives for an ideal. There is also no more savage and brutally cruel people, no people readier in their weakness to betray their nearest and dearest for their own safety.

The British are the people of the middle way. The Russians despise compromise, and their favourite Biblical quotation is from Revelations, Chapter III, verse 16: 'So then because thou art lukewarm and neither cold nor hot, I will spue thee out of my mouth.'

The destructive element in the Russian character appears at all periods in Russian history and reveals itself in the form of palace revolutions, imperial murders, inhuman indifference to life and savage revolts against the Tsarist rule of nationalism, orthodoxy and authoritarianism.

The first of these revolts to have any influence on the revolutions of 1917 goes back to 1667 when Stenka Razin, a Don Cossack, raised an army of serfs, poor Cossacks, gaol-birds, and discontented elements from the towns. In those times the Cossacks were accustomed to make piratical expeditions against the Turks and Tartars, and Stenka Razin's revolt started as a raid on the Persian coast of the Caspian Sea. His success not only roused his political ambitions, but stirred the whole of south-east Russia. On his promise of liberty and equality to all, thousands flocked to his standard. In 1670 he took Tsaritsyn. A year later Astrakhan, Saratov and Samara were in his hands. His name and fame became legendary, and in his tracks serfs slew their owners. The whole Tsarist state was shaken, and it was not until 1671 that the Tsarist generals, with the aid of foreign troops, were able to defeat his army in a bloody battle at Simbirsk, the birthplace of Vladimir Ilyich Ulianov-Lenin and now called Ulianovsk after him.

Razin, himself an illiterate and bloodthirsty savage, was handed over by his defeated troops to the Tsarist commander, taken to Moscow and tortured and quartered on the Red Square. But the legend of his exploits lived on in the memory of the down-trodden and oppressed.

Even today the most popular song from Brest to Vladivostok is still the ballad in which Stenka Razin, accused of weakness because he has taken to himself a captured Russian princess, rises from his semi-drunken orgy, seizes his bride and hurls her into the river with the words: 'Volga, Volga, Mother Volga, Behold the gift of the Don Cossack.'

It is perhaps typically Russian that before the First World War and, indeed, up to the Bolshevik Revolution every *bourgeois* and every noble not only knew all eighteen verses of the ballad by heart but, when warmed by vodka or wine in a restaurant, insisted on its being played by the orchestra.

More relevant to the influence of Stenka Razin is the fact that Gorky, in one of his earlier stories, describes the ecstasy of his hero, the drunken vagabond Konovalov, on having the story of Stenka Razin read to him. Gorky adds the comment: 'It seemed as if the ties of blood, still not cut after three centuries, bound this vagabond to Stenka, for with his whole body, living and robust, and with the whole passion of his mind he felt the anguish and the anger of a free falcon captured three hundred years ago.'

Almost exactly a hundred years after the death of Razin, Emilian Pugachev, also an illiterate Don Cossack, raised another revolt in the area between the Volga and the Ural rivers. By posing as Peter III, the murdered husband of Catherine the Great, and by promising freedom and the land to the serfs, he attracted to his army not only peasants but also valuable recruits from the Bashkirs, Kalmucks, Kirghiz and other non-Slavic peoples of the area. Arson and pillage marked his trail. Wherever he went, the serfs refused to work for their masters, and sometimes murdered them and burned their houses. In 1774 Pugachev took Kazan and could have threatened Moscow. Instead, he fell back on the Volga towns, and gradually Catherine's troops, led by the subsequently famous Suvorov, surrounded him. Like Stenka Razin, he was handed over by his own troops, taken to Moscow in a cage and executed.

The ghastly murders committed by his troops and camp-followers provoked the most brutal reprisals, and from now onwards relations between landowner and serf were to be marked by hate and suspicion. Lenin, who was born almost a hundred years after the Pugachev revolt, made a careful study of all the subversive movements in Russian history. From the Pugachev revolt he learnt for the first time how easy it was to work on the mind of the Russian peasantry and to rouse them from individual docile resignation to collective cruelty of the most brutal nature. If illiterate rascals like Stenka Razin and Pugachev could make the Russian throne tremble, what could he himself, a professional revolutionary, not achieve by scientific leadership?

Today the Soviet leaders refer to the dead Lenin as their authority for collective leadership as opposed to the cult of the individual, but in his life-time Lenin himself never tried to hide his intention of being the master of the Bolshevik Party, and three years after he had achieved power he said quite openly: 'Soviet social democracy is not in the least incompatible with individual rule and dictatorship. ... What is necessary is individual rule, the recognition of the dictatorial powers of one man.'

Up to the reign of Peter the Great (1682–1725) Russia was a weak, backward, savage country more Asian than European. When he came to the throne, the population of Russia was not much more than 14 millions or approximately two-thirds of the then population of France. The masses were kept in profound ignorance of the outside world, and no citizen was allowed to leave the country without the permission of the Patriarch. This ban, as Voltaire relates, was based on the fear that a journey abroad might reveal to the Russian traveller the miserable lot of his countrymen at home.

In his desire for radical change and in his belief in his own infallibility and in personal dictatorship Peter was as much a revolutionary as Lenin. In an even higher degree he possessed the same ruthlessness and the same determination to destroy whatever obstacle stood in his way. The building of St Petersburg on the swamps of the Neva cost thousands of lives, but it opened the famous 'window on Europe'. He found an army quite unfit to stand up to European armies. In his first great battle against Charles XII of Sweden at Narva, 50,000 Russians were scattered like chaff by 8,000 Swedes.

Relying on that defence in depth which has so often saved Russia from defeat, he created new armies, engaged foreign generals to lead them, enforced a discipline which would have made even Germans shudder and defeated all his enemies, including the Cossacks and other elements of his own subjects who had risen against him.

Peter had the typical Russian passion for the extreme in all things. He worked prodigiously; he ate and drank enormously; he trampled violently on ancient traditions and superstitions; he praised exultantly; he could be fiercely suspicious, and his rages were like a thunderstorm; he was abnormally cruel. Two hundred years later he was to serve as a model and a hero to Stalin.

There were other traits in Peter's character which appealed to the ruthlessness of the modern Bolsheviks. He trusted no one. When General Patrick Gordon, who saved the throne and whom Peter loved as a brother, wished to go back to Scotland for a holiday, Peter retained his wife and family as hostages to ensure his safe return. He had also no regard for religious superstitions and did not hesitate to put the Church in what he thought was its place. He introduced into Russia the habit of smoking which hitherto had been forbidden by the Church because Holy Writ said: 'Not that which goeth into the mouth defileth man; but that which cometh out of the mouth defileth man.' On the same reasoning the Russian *muzhik* was allowed to drink spirits till he dropped. Peter's revolution was national and patriotic, and it came from above.

If the Stenka Razin and Pugachev adventures were based on a revolt of the masses, the next revolutionary movement came from a very different quarter. On the death of the Tsar Alexander I, his younger brother Constantine should have succeeded, but, having married a commoner, he refused the throne in favour of the third brother, Nicholas. There was some delay in the signing of the abdication and during this period the liberal-minded officers of the Imperial Guard plotted to refuse allegiance to Nicholas and to demand the throne for Constantine, the lawful Tsar. The day on which Nicholas was to be proclaimed Emperor was December 26, 1825, but when the guards regiments went to take the oath of allegiance, something went wrong with the plot, for only one regiment refused. Three times Nicholas sent emissaries to persuade the regiment to submit, but all were met with rifle fire, and several were killed. As the mob was now showing signs of joining the insurgents, artillery was brought up and order was restored. Because of the date, the insurgents, who included in their number some of the noblest names in Russia, were known as the Decembrists. In all 579 were arrested. Of these five paid with their lives, others received long sentences and many were exiled to Siberia.

The main articles of their programme were: (1) abolition of serfdom; (2) equality of all citizens before the law; (3) reform of justice; (4) establishment of a parliamentary régime and (5) control of public expenditure. Other reforms, such as the abolition of Tsarism and the proclamation of a Republic, were not included because complete agreement could not be reached on these points. To us today these reforms may seem almost elementary, but Russia had to wait a long time for them, and some have never been effectively realised. They were, in fact, the first social reforms ever put forward by the upper class in Russia, and the result was disastrous. The revolt confirmed the Emperor Nicholas in his belief in absolutism. It also split the Russian Empire into two sharply divided groups in which the autocratic Tsarist Government with its rich landowning class and its vast bureaucracy, including the officers of the armed forces, was arrayed against the intelligentsia composed mainly of professors, writers, students, professional men and members of the educated urban population, and the inert, disorganised masses of the serfs.

During the reign of Nicholas I (1825–55) Tsardom held the upper hand. The population of Russia in Europe and of Siberia had now grown to 50 millions, of which 25 millions were serfs of the landowners and 20 millions were peasants of the state and its appanages. Not more than ten per cent of the people could read or write. Up to the First World War the shops, even in the main streets of St Petersburg and Moscow, had, in addition to the names of their owners, painted signs portraying a loaf of bread, a cube of sugar or a ham in order that the illiterate might know where and what to buy.

If the peasantry could on occasion be roused to extreme violence, they were prone to relapse into long periods of extreme resignation. Distances between villages were great, and the secret police were everywhere. In peace-time subversion was well-nigh impossible. Only a war in which Russia was engaged could permit organised revolt and put the necessary arms into the hands of the people. Throughout Russian history nearly all the great revolts have taken place when the government was engaged in foreign wars.

Throughout his reign Nicholas I continued to impose and strengthen the policy of absolutism. Education was cut down. The teaching of philosophy was forbidden and the numbers of schools and universities reduced. Travel abroad was heavily restricted, and newspapers and letters were severely censored. Alarmed by the revolutionary movements of the year 1848, Nicholas sent Russian troops abroad to quell the Hungarian rising.

In spite of the dead hand of absolutism the reign was rich in the arts and especially in literature. It was the period of Pushkin and Lermontov, Russia's two greatest poets, both of whom were killed in duels before they were forty. It also saw the birth of Gogol's *Dead Souls* and the débuts of Turgenev, Nekrasov and Dostoyevsky. On December 22, 1849, Dostoyevsky narrowly escaped execution for complicity in the Petra-shevsky conspiracy of ideas. He was already in his shirt before the scaffold when the reprieve arrived.

Politically the reign was notable for the intellectual struggle between the Slavophils and the Westerners. The former exalted the Orthodox Church and sought to regenerate Russia by building upon her national traditions. They wanted the peasants, the backbone of Russia, to live prosperously in their rural communities under the benign rule of a popular mon-archy. They were sceptical of Western industrialism and constitutionalism. The Westerners believed that progress could best be achieved by closer association with Europe. Their out-look was more secular. Politically, they were republicans and liberals, or in some cases socialists. Neither Slavophils nor Westerners cared much for the doctrines of economic *laissez-faire*. After 1848 Alexander Herzen combined elements from both schools of thought to form an influential creed that came to be called 'Populism'. This asserted that Russia could find her own way to socialism, based upon the peasants' collective spirit, and avoid the horrors of Western-style capitalism.

The peasants, however, remained in a state of resigned sub-jection. They were not yet politically minded and, as Belinsky wrote, 'they had a desire for potatoes and none at all for a constitution; the latter is wanted by the educated urban classes who are powerless to do anything.'

The Emperor Nicholas ended his reign in sorrow and despair. Having engaged himself in the Crimean War which, however badly conducted by France and Great Britain, went still worse for Russia, he died of chagrin and disappointment. Although he maintained the autocracy unimpaired, he left a heavy legacy to his son, Alexander II.

From now on the struggle between the absolutists and the reformers was to be waged with increasing bitterness. It was to be marked by the liberation of the serfs, the movement of the educated classes to enlighten the peasants, and, most im-portant of all, the emergence of a proletariat as the result of the Russian industrial revolution, created largely by German, British and French enterprise and capital.

2

The Russia of the Tsars

THE reign of Alexander II (1855–81) was in many respects the
most tragic in Russian history, for he was the best-intentioned
and the most intelligent of all the Tsars. Thirty-seven years of
age when he ascended the throne, he was a man of great good
looks, superb stature and noble character. His first act was to
terminate the unhappy Crimean War. The Treaty of Paris put
an end for a time to Russia's hopes of asserting her influence
in south-eastern Europe, but gave her peace and time to deal
with the internal unrest which an unsuccessful war had created.
Not without reason the bulk of the educated people attributed
the Russian defeat to the tyranny and incompetence of absolutism.

In announcing the peace, the Tsar promised a series of reforms,
and in 1856 urged the nobility to help work out a scheme to
emancipate the serfs. But most nobles and the high officials
expressed their horror and predicted inevitable disaster, and
owing to their opposition five years passed before the emancipation became law. It gave the peasants personal freedom but
imposed upon them very heavy economic burdens. Not enough
was done to promote agricultural progress. The peasants
generally felt that they had been cheated of possession of all
the land, which should by rights belong to those who worked
it by their labour.

Both before and after the emancipation of the serfs the
Emperor promulgated numerous other liberal reforms, of which
the most important was the institution of the provincial
Zemstvos which, although controlled by the provincial
Governor, had some of the functions of the British county
council. Female education was introduced; the number of
schools multiplied; the pre-publication censorship of newspapers and reviews was relaxed; and a modern judicial system
was introduced with independent judges and trial by jury.

Unfortunately, the liberalism of the Emperor antagonised the reactionaries and merely whetted the appetite of the fanatical radical elements. By curbing absolutism the Emperor had unwittingly unloosed the greatest wave of revolutionary radicalism that Russia had ever seen.

In 1862, one year after the emancipation of the serfs, a secret revolutionary society, called Land and Liberty, was formed. Most of its members were educated young men and women. Driven by frustrated idealism and egged on by famous revolutionary exiles such as Herzen or Bakunin, they endeavoured to spread Populist agrarian socialism among the peasants. But their efforts were soon cut short by the police. Some of the 'more extreme revolutionaries, whom their opponents called 'nihilists', denied the value of all accepted social institutions—religion, art and even the family—except in so far as they could be made to serve what they thought were the best interests of society. The authorities, worried by the spread of these dangerous ideas, began to tighten the controls. The revolutionaries responded by acts of terror and assassination. On April 16, 1866, a young fanatic called Karakozov met the Emperor in his daily walk in the Summer Garden in St Petersburg and fired a pistol at him almost pointblank. He missed. Nevertheless, it was the first attempt by a revolutionary against the life of a Tsar. It was followed by numerous other and more successful efforts. It has always been said that if a would-be assassin of normal education and ability is prepared to give his own life he can succeed in killing his victim. In the state of exultation which the members of the secret societies had reached there were scores of young men and women who were consumed by a fanatical desire to take life by sacrificing their own. Public opinion admired their courage, and when, in February, 1878, Vera Zasulich severely wounded the Chief of Police in St Petersburg, she was tried by jury and acquitted amid scenes of great enthusiasm.

The terror and the mania for assassination were intensified by the Russo-Turkish War of 1877–8 which, started as a Russian effort to support an insurrection of the Balkan peoples against the Turks, brought some prestige, but little profit to

Russia. The Emperor had been opposed to the war, but had been forced into it by the wild enthusiasm of the Panslavs who already saw the Cross standing on the cupola of Saint Sophia. Constantinople, however, was denied to Russia, and at home the heavy losses and a serious financial crisis added greatly to the existing discontent.

By now the society of Land and Liberty had given way to a still more violent secret organisation called The People's Will. It was administered by a secret Executive Committee whose members chose not only the victims, but also the assassins for the next political murder. It was typical of the fanaticism among these revolutionary terrorists that many of them were willing to carry out their grim tasks without complaint.

In spite of several attempts on his life Alexander II had by no means abandoned his wish to reform. To his Zemstvos or county councils he had added municipal councils, and even after the end of the Russo-Turkish War he began to develop with his chief minister, Loris-Melikov, ideas for reforming the central government. A plan was drawn up for a commission to advise the Tsar and his State Council on forthcoming bills, some members of which were to be elected by the Zemstvos and municipal councils. The proposal did not restrict the autocratic prerogatives of the Tsar or introduce a parliamentary system of government, but if it had been acted upon it would have been a great step forward in the direction of constitutional democracy.

On the morning of March 13, 1881, the Emperor, who had assented to the plan, approved a draft statement announcing it to the public. That day was a Sunday, and, because of police reports of new plots, Loris-Melikov begged the Emperor to put off his weekly review of the Imperial Guards. Alexander II was not the man to stay at home for fear. Like Winston Churchill, he was a fatalist. On his way back from the review a young man threw a packet into his carriage. There was a loud explosion. The horses and two Cossacks were killed and others wounded. But Alexander was unhurt. As he went to help the wounded, another young man threw a second bomb straight at the Emperor. His huge frame collapsed, and he was dead before he could be brought back to his Palace. Had the bomb failed to explode, there was another assassin near by who had a third bomb with which, if necessary, to finish off the ghastly job. It was Sophie Perovskaya, a woman of noble family who as a girl of nineteen had 'gone to the people', and, after several months of imprisonment, had joined The People's Will. She was the first woman to be hanged in Russia. According to the statistics of arrests for revolutionary activities up to the death of Alexander II, the nobility with fifty-five per cent was by far the highest group.

Prince Kropotkin, the anarchist, whom I met in Russia, knew Sophie Perovskaya and recounts how she told him: 'We have undertaken a secret task. Two generations may succumb before it is finished. Nevertheless, it must be accomplished.'

Her prophecy of two generations was exact. At the time of Alexander's murder a young boy called Vladimir Ilyich Ulianov was within six weeks of his eleventh birthday. In later life he took the name of Lenin—after his place of banishment in Siberia, near the Lena River.

Alexander II was succeeded by his second son, Alexander III, who was prepared to go ahead with his father's reforms including the promulgation of the Consultative Commission. The murder of the Tsar Liberator, however, had created a strong reaction against the terrorists, whose punishment was accepted by the public without much protest. Moreover, the new Tsar was very much under the influence of his former tutor, Pobedonostsev, who was the high priest of absolutism and who, although only holding the post of Procurator of the Holy Synod, was in practice the new Emperor's chief minister.

His first action was to reorganise both the official and the secret police and to establish all over Europe a network of spies to control the movements of the revolutionaries abroad. High on the list of useful informers were the *agents-provocateurs*.

Under his firm rule the police system was reorganised. A network of spies controlled the movement of the revolutionaries abroad. *Agents-provocateurs* were employed to break the secret terrorist organisations. Life became increasingly difficult for The People's Will, and most of its members were either arrested or decided to go into exile. Some of those who remained at liberty plotted to assassinate the new Emperor on March 13, 1887, the sixth anniversary of the murder of his father. Before they could put their plan into execution, they were arrested. Among the ringleaders was Alexander Ulianov, elder brother of Lenin, and he and fourteen others were brought to trial. Alexander behaved with high courage, seeking to assume the whole blame and declaring with his last words: 'Terror is our answer to the violence of the state. It is the only way to force a despotic régime to grant political freedom to the people.' He was hanged on May 20, 1887, and his death had undoubtedly a strong influence on the future career of his younger brother, Vladimir, who was just seventeen at the time.

In spite of their belief in acts of terror, the members of The People's Will were idealists who hoped that, once Tsarism was removed, Utopia would come by itself. They had no thought of a dictatorship of the proletariat or of establishing minority rule. They were not much interested in Marxism which was just beginning to take root in Russia. The first Russian Marxist society was founded abroad in 1883 by Plekhanov and Axelrod, and its main function was to propagate the doctrine that socialism could never be established by a peasant revolt, but only by an organised and class-conscious proletariat.

By severe police supervision and by diverting Russian mob violence to pogroms against Jews the autocracy maintained order, and Alexander III's reign was the first for a century in which there was no war. Meanwhile, the Empire had been expanding both territorially and industrially. During Alexander III's reign the railways had been extended by fifty per cent, thereby promoting the mining and metallurgical industries. The ever-increasing textile factories round Moscow and St Petersburg were attracting more and more countrymen and, although the percentage of industrial workers was tiny in relation to the whole population, a total of a million and a quarter workers, concentrated in the four or five industrial cities of the Empire, constituted quite a formidable proletarian force.

Foreign commerce, too, had increased from 276 million

roubles in 1855 to more than a milliard in 1891. New territories had been won by conquest in Central Asia, and efforts were being made to colonise Siberia. Agriculture made slower progress, and owing to lack of sufficient transport rarely a year passed without some part of Russia suffering from famine. When Alexander III died in November, 1894, Russia was emerging from a purely agricultural country into a semi-modern capitalist and industrial state.

Since 1917 it has been the habit of the Communists to describe the Russia of the Tsars as a kind of desert which left the country 300 years behind the rest of the world. In point of fact, industrial and commercial progress was exceedingly rapid from 1884 right up to 1914.

The Emperors Alexander II and III had been, in their different manner, men of strong character and firm determination. Nicholas II, who succeeded his father, Alexander III, in 1894 had all the characteristics of a weak ruler. He could be obstinate when he should have been yielding. He was invariably feeble when he should have shown strength. Throughout his tragic life he was dominated by his wife, the Empress Alexandra Feodorovna, daughter of the Grand Duke of Hesse and grand-daughter of Queen Victoria. The Empress's mother died when her daughter was only six years old, and from then onwards Queen Victoria brought her up and supervised her education. She was therefore much more English in outlook than German. Yet in the years of tragedy she was to be labelled 'Nemka' (the German) by the Russian masses. In character she was a pious and devoted woman, but much oppressed by lugubrious forebodings and only too ready to be swayed by superstitions which made her an easy prey for pseudo-religious charlatans.

On ascending the throne the Emperor Nicholas, with the insistent Pobedonostsev at his elbow, did little more than repeat the words of his father. The dreams of the reformers were 'senseless'. He would not relinquish one whit of the divine authority which God had given him.

The reign began with one of those disasters which arouse the worst superstitions of an illiterate people. During the coronation celebrations in Moscow on May 30, 1896, there was a vast open-air fête for the peasants on Khodynka Field outside the city. The fact that souvenir cups were to be given to all developed into the rumour that every peasant was to receive a present of a cow. The peasants, therefore, rushed forward in order to be in the front rank. The police, whose precautions were inadequate, were swept aside, and in the crush that ensued over 1,000 peasants were trampled to death. On his way back to Moscow, the Imperial carriage passed the hay-carts carrying the corpses, and the Emperor is said to have remarked: 'This bodes no good for my reign.'

The same evening the Emperor and Empress, who were doubtless slaves of the ceremonial protocol of their own Court, attended a ball given by the French ambassador.

The nation was shocked and blamed the Empress. The superstitious masses saw the worst omens for a reign which had begun with such a disaster.

For the moment, however, Russia, under the guidance of Sergey Witte, who had risen from a minor post on the railways to become Alexander III's Minister of Finance, continued to make economic progress, and the modernisation of the country proceeded apace, thanks mainly to French loans negotiated by Witte. In 1898 Russia had become the fourth country of the world for the production of steel and iron, and work was going ahead on the great Trans-Siberian Railway. Polytechnical institutes and commercial academies were springing up in the major cities. In 1897, after a strike in the textile mills of St Petersburg, the working day in industry was regulated—at eleven and a half hours.

For the workers the prospects of sharing in the fruits of future industrial prosperity seemed remote when compared with their present grim conditions. They were more and more ready to listen to Marxist revolutionary agitators. In March, 1898, a small congress was held at Minsk which formally proclaimed the foundation of the Russian Social-Democratic Workers' Party. The new party was created from tiny Marxist groups, of which the Jewish Bund, founded in 1897, was the most important. During the next nineteen years the Social-

Democrats were to be harried by the Government, driven into exile or sent to Siberia, and riven by internal squabbles. Peter Struve, who wrote the manifesto and whom I was to meet later in Moscow, recanted and renounced his Socialism. Lenin, who was then serving his only period of enforced exile in Siberia, had no part in the foundation of the party. But from this organised group sprang the Mensheviks and the Bolsheviks. March 1898 is the first date in the history of Bolshevism.

3

The Rise of Lenin

THE early history of Russian Social-Democracy is compli-
cated by the existence of groups of different tendencies and by
squabbles over theory at the expense of leadership and organ-
ising ability. Groups like the Economists concentrated their
efforts on the economic interests of the workers. At the other
extreme was the League for the Liberation of Labour, which
demanded a fighting policy and no compromise.

Three names are connected with the Marxist movement in
Russia. They are Plekhanov, the Father of Russian Social-
Democracy, Martov, subsequently leader of the Mensheviks,
and, greatest of all, Lenin, the uncompromising leader, with-
out whose capacity for work, iron determination and supreme
self-confidence Communist Russia might never have existed.
Plekhanov, an anti-terrorist, was the philosopher of Marxism.
Lenin was the man of action.

Vladimir Ilyich Ulianov-Lenin was born in Simbirsk, a
Volga town which also gave birth to Alexander Kerensky. His
parents were highly respected and conventional citizens. His
father was the chief inspector of schools for the province and,
as in Russia high rank in the armed forces and civil service
led automatically to admission to the *dvorianstvo*, or nobility,
Lenin père was entered on his passport as *dvorianin*, or noble-
man. The rank was hereditary. His mother, whose maiden
name was Blank and who was the daughter of a doctor, had
German as well as Russian blood in her veins.

Lenin's father was a close friend of Kerensky's father, the
director of the local secondary school, and in his will he
appointed Kerensky's father as guardian of the Ulianov family.

Lenin, who had begun to read Marx when he was seventeen, went to Kazan University and was expelled in his first
term, seven months after his brother Alexander had been
hanged. Through his mother's influence he was eventually able

to pass his law examinations at the University of St Petersburg, and in 1893 he took up his residence in the capital and at once joined a secret society. Two years later he went abroad for reasons of health after pneumonia and in Geneva he met Plekhanov. As Lenin was still learning, Plekhanov formed a high opinion of his new disciple, and nothing could have been further from his mind than the thought that one day Lenin would sweep him from his path as he destroyed everyone who opposed him.

Back again in St Petersburg in September, 1895, Lenin was arrested three months later and, after serving his sentence in prison, was banished in 1897 for three years to Siberia. They were not unprofitable or even unhappy years. Nadezhda Krupskaya, who became his wife, joined him at Shushenskye, his Siberian village, and together they wrote books and articles and translated Sidney and Beatrice Webb's *Theory and Practice of Trade Unionism*. In comparison with the Communist prison camps, banishment under the Tsarist régime was mild. Letters and books arrived regularly. Lenin played chess with other exiled Social-Democrats and, as his Siberian letters show, thoroughly enjoyed the hunting and fishing trips which he was allowed to undertake unaccompanied.

Freed in 1900, he made his way abroad via St Petersburg. In Siberia he had written *The Aims of Russian Social Democrats*. From Munich he was now to produce the newspaper *Iskra* or *The Spark*, which was not only to propagate Marxism in Russia but also to advocate the kind of party organisation which he himself wanted. Always opposed to any form of compromise, he stood full-front for the dictatorship of the proletariat, although at that time he saw it as a sequel to a preliminary *bourgeois* revolution.

In 1902 difficulties over the printing of his newspaper in Munich drove him to London where he worked at the British Museum. In London, too, he met the young Trotsky who impressed Lenin more favourably than Lenin at first impressed him.

During this period the Russian Social-Democrat exiles were scattered, Lenin being in London and Plekhanov and Axelrod

27

having their headquarters in Switzerland. As Lenin wanted his way in all matters, misunderstandings and disagreements became frequent. In April, 1903, Lenin and Krupskaya went to Switzerland in order to prepare for the Party Congress which had been instigated by *Iskra* and for which delegates from Russia itself were beginning to assemble in Switzerland. The Congress was to be the show-down between the extremists led by Lenin and the moderates who preferred democratic methods to dictatorship and who were led by Martov.

The Congress opened in Brussels on July 30, 1903, but, owing to the interference of the Belgian police, it was transferred to London. Here forty-three delegates assembled, and here was fought the battle which split the Social-Democrats into the two sections of Mensheviks and Bolsheviks.

Even before the Congress was mooted, Lenin's mind was clear. He wanted a revolutionary general staff of which he would be the sole boss, the control of *Iskra* over the whole party and the acceptance of his belief that no revolution could succeed unless it was led by the proletariat, prepared and disciplined by a body of professional revolutionaries. As was his custom, he had worked out the procedure beforehand with Plekhanov as chairman and himself as one of the two vice-chairmen, and, as usual, he refused to compromise.

The actual resolution which led to the breach was on the proposal that membership of the party should be restricted to professional revolutionaries, and on this issue Lenin was defeated. But on all other resolutions he won easily, and as his faction had the majority or *bolshinstvo* and the Martov group the minority or *menshinstvo*, the two factions were labelled *Bolsheviki* and *Mensheviki*.

The Congress ended unharmoniously with the delegates barely on speaking terms. A further meeting in Geneva produced still greater acrimony, and Lenin, accused of trying to keep *Iskra* for himself, resigned the editorship.

His conduct came in for severe condemnation from his former colleagues. Plekhanov, who later was to disagree with him, gave him full support, but the Mensheviks accused him of autocratic methods, and Trotsky, still in his twenties, described him with a pen of vitriol as a terrorist and despot who wished to establish a dictatorship, not of the proletariat, but over it. Later, President Masaryk was to make a similar remark.

At the time of the Congress Lenin was just thirty-three and at his most vigorous. Short of stature and bald, but sturdily built with high-domed forehead and Mongolian features, he had an immense capacity for work. He had a keen sense of humour and was above all personal hates. But on the subject of revolution he was adamant. He knew that, for revolution to be successful, fighting and civil war were necessary, and he despised and characterised as *bourgeois* the humanitarianism of leaders such as Plekhanov or Martov who believed that without political freedom Social Democracy would degenerate into autocracy and urged that the coming revolution should be the work of the masses themselves, not of a small group which spoke in their name. Although Lenin advocated collective leadership of the party, in fact he brooked no opposition. Not only did he believe in the necessity of force; he also accepted the theory that a good end justified the worst means. In this respect his views were much nearer Nechaev's than Herzen's, and he agreed fully with Nechaev's concept of the revolutionary as a man who lives for one purpose only: to destroy the existing social order by any means that he can command.

Echoing Nechaev's philosophy, Lenin himself was to write later: 'A Communist must be prepared to make every sacrifice and, if necessary, even resort to all sorts of schemes and stratagems, employ illegitimate methods, conceal the truth, in order to get into the trade unions, stay there, and conduct the revolutionary work within. . . .'

He did not consider this as immoral. On the contrary, he justified it by the immorality of *bourgeois* ethics. 'We repudiate,' he wrote, 'all morality that is taken out of human class concepts. We say that this is deception, a fraud, which clogs the brains of the workers and peasants in the interests of the landlords and the capitalists. We say that our morality is entirely subordinated to the interest of the class struggle of the proletariat. . . .

'And what is this class struggle? It is the overthrow of the Tsar and of the capitalists and the destruction of the capitalist class.'

His legal training and his profound study of Marx made him a brilliant dialectician, but his greatest strength was his immense will-power. Feeling that he had a mission in life, he believed himself infallible, and, thus armed, he lambasted his opponents with a vigour of self-confidence and an unceasing flow of sarcastic argument which few could withstand. Not so brilliant an orator as Trotsky, he could quell an angry crowd, partly by his skill in diverting their attention from their grievances, but mainly by his ability to impress them with a profound sense of his own personal superiority. Nationalism meant less than nothing to him, and the great part of his adult life was spent out of Russia. Revolution was in his blood and he thought and dreamt of it for part of every day and night.

He took no interest in drama or in literature unless it had some bearing on the class struggle. He admired Tolstoy's *The Living Corpse* and Barbusse's *The Fire*. He gave high praise to Gorky for his revolutionary writings, but found his *The Lower Depths* too theatrical. He detested Dickens, the most popular of all English writers among Russians today, for 'his middle-class sentimentality' and, although he liked Jack London's *Love of Life*, he discarded his other works as boringly *bourgeois*. On the other hand, he loved the open air and was a keen cyclist until he ran into a tram in Geneva and was nearly killed. Above all, he was a great 'hiker', and after the stress and storm of the London Congress his wife and he made a long and happy walking tour through Switzerland. Her account of it shows that on such occasions he could not only relax, but also be very human and almost boyish. Like Winston Churchill's, his married life was happy and beyond reproach.

In conversation with a foreigner he was self-possessed, polite and remarkably frank. Better educated and less self-conscious than many Communist leaders today, he was always at his ease and could on occasion be mildly humorous. But his opinions were as firm as steel and to attempt to make him modify them was like a child trying to swim against a tidal wave. The argument whether the event makes the man or the man makes the event is beside the point. Lenin was essentially not the man to miss the event, for which, since his brother's death, he had prepared with confidence.

The event came more suddenly than he expected. After the split in the Social-Democratic Party he had not fared too well. Although both Mensheviks and Bolsheviks recognised in him the enviable twin talents of a brilliant theorist and a practical organiser, they were afraid of his extremism and of his contempt for other movements and parties and regarded him as a young man in a hurry. Plekhanov, jealous of a formidable rival, had already formed reservations about him, and, apart from Lenin himself, the Mensheviks had all the big names.

Moreover, Lenin had lost *Iskra* and a newspaper had to be launched to take its place. The Bolshevik writers gave their services for nothing, but even so the smallest news-sheet eats money. Where was the money to be found? In Russia it is always the unexpected which happens. Through Gorky Lenin came into contact with 'Savva' Morozov, a millionaire textile-manufacturer who was interested in Socialism. Well prepared by the genial and suave Krasin, then Bolshevik financial expert and later Soviet ambassador in London, he was attracted by Lenin's arguments and, not least perhaps, by his magnetism, and the result was a small but regular subsidy for the next year or two until in 1905 Morozov committed suicide. In his will he left a considerable sum to the Bolshevik Party. He was not the only rich manufacturer to finance the Bolsheviks. In 1905 a Moscow industrialist called Schmidt, who tried to institute co-partnership for his workers, left over 100,000 roubles to the Central Committee of the party.

Nevertheless, in spite of this windfall which helped to create the new newspaper, *Forward*, Lenin contemplated rather grimly the prospect of a long period of propaganda to educate the semi-literate Russian proletariat. The long desired revolution still seemed far away, even though discontent among Russian workers was increasing rapidly at this time. There was also trouble among the peasants, but those who made the most of this were not the Marxist Social-Democrats but the Socialist-Revolutionaries, who took up again the Populist tradition of the old People's Will group. They maintained a terrorist organisation headed first by a young scientist named Gershuni and later by Azev, an *agent-provocateur* who served both the revolutionaries and the police. From time to time these men arranged the assassination of a minister of the interior or the governor of a province. By way of diverting the attention of the masses from revolutionary propaganda, the Government encouraged anti-Semitism and undoubtedly played a part in the organisations of pogroms, thereby encouraging the lust and savagery of the mob.

In spite of these unpleasant excitements the country was relatively quiet. Ever since the murder of Alexander II the public mind had become blunt to sensationalism and accepted occasional assassinations and the odd pogrom as a normal part of daily life. As for Lenin, he was not interested in ministerial murders or in the educated young men and women who, knowing nothing of the land, went off to the country to talk down to the peasants. He believed in action from above down to the bottom; in civil war and revolution rather than in single murders and rural arson.

Then out of a more or less serene sky came the thunderclap. Encouraged by the German Kaiser, who appealed to Nicholas's deep sense of Christianity, the Tsar blundered into war with Japan. The fault was not entirely his. The war was the result of the expansionist policy adopted by some of his ministers and advisers, who, not for the first time, regarded a successful colonial or minor war as an excellent antidote to trouble at home.

By way of contrast, even during the Crimean War revolutionaries like Herzen and Bakunin had hoped for the defeat of Russia. Since then it had become an axiom of the Russian revolutionaries that defeat of their own country was the essential prelude to a successful revolution, and by the turn of the century not only the Social-Democrats and Socialist-Revolutionaries, but also some of the Liberals shared this view.

Hostilities began on February 8, 1904. From the beginning, the Russian forces, operating 4,000 miles from their bases on a single railway-line, were at a hopeless disadvantage, and, as the news of successive defeats by land and sea reached the home front, the revolutionary ardour of the people rose until it spilled over in action.

4

Dress Rehearsal—1905

THE efforts of the autocracy to stave off revolution by economic progress and by expansion in Asia did little to solve the social and political problems which, to the exclusion of all else, exercised the mind of the Liberals and the various socialist factions. From the first Russian defeat in the Far East anti-Tsarist feeling began to ferment throughout the country, and in July, 1904, Plehve, the reactionary Minister of the Interior, was assassinated. In November of the same year a Congress of the Zemstvos (County Councils) recommended among other reforms a parliamentary régime and freedom of conscience, speech and assembly. A month later the Tsar, apparently changing course as the result of public excitement, invited the Council of Ministers to study the possibilities of extending the rights of the Zemstvos and to consider what other reforms could be granted.

What really gave the signal for the revolution of 1905 was the fall of Port Arthur which, after what seemed to be a heroic resistance, capitulated tamely when a sortie by the Russian Far Eastern Fleet ended disastrously. Strikes broke out in St Petersburg. A petition requesting basic civil liberties, a constituent assembly, an eight-hour day and other reforms was signed by over a hundred thousand workers, and arrangements were made for it to be presented to the Tsar by a monster procession headed by Father Gapon, an Orthodox priest and rather mysterious figure who, though opposed to all violence, enjoyed the confidence of the people and, if not actually supported by the secret police, was tolerated by them.

At this time Lenin was in Geneva busily considering how to implement an offer by Maxim Gorky, who had undertaken to collect and give the Bolshevik Party all the profits from a foreign edition of his works and those of other like-minded Russian Socialist writers. Gorky himself was then in St Petersburg, and his diary gives a graphic account of the course of events. On January 19, 1905, he sends to Lenin a cheque for 3,000 roubles (*circa* £300) for his new journal, *Forward*, and the transaction is duly noted and entered in the day-book of the Department of Police.

As is usual in illiterate countries, rumour goes farther and deeper among the masses than any written word. On January 21 the story spreads like fire through the city that the workers will not be allowed to approach the Tsar and that troops are being concentrated round the Winter Palace. The same day Gorky organises a small deputation to go immediately to Count Witte and the Chief of the Gendarmerie in order to urge them to avoid at all cost a collision of the workers with the soldiery. When Witte says that 'the opinion of the ruling spheres differs irreconcilably from yours', Gorky replies: 'We propose that you inform the ruling sphere that, if blood flows tomorrow, they will pay dearly for it.'

The next day each side follows its own will. As usual, there is no compromise. The workers, led by Father Gapon, some carrying crosses and portraits of the Tsar, converge on the Palace Square. An officer orders them to disperse. There is a moment's hesitation. Then the troops fire. The fusillade kills over a hundred victims and wounds several hundred more.

Gorky, an eye-witness, writes: 'January 22, 1905. From early morning I was in the streets, saw how they shot and mowed down the people, saw the miserable figure of the crumpled leader and "hero of the hour" Gapon. . . . Everything was cut short and smashed on that accursed, but instructive day.'

The same evening he writes to a friend: 'I believe that this is the beginning of the end of the blood-thirsty Tsar.' In a letter to his wife, he instructs her to inform another revolutionary friend: 'Tell him that a future historian will probably begin his work with the phrase: "The first day of the Russian Revolution was the day of the moral collapse of the Russian intelligentsia".' Like Lenin, Gorky had no faith in the Liberals. Unconsciously perhaps, he preferred another autocrat in Lenin.

A foreign witness, Maurice Paléologue, who was the French ambassador in Russia during the First World War and wrote several excellent and indispensable books on the period from 1855 to 1917, agrees with Gorky as to the importance of the date. In *The Precursors of Lenin* he wrote: 'The date of January 22, 1905, marks a tragic turning in the history of the Romanovs.'

There can, in fact, be no other opinion. Had the Tsar received the petition, promised to consider it and then sent the crowd away with a few kind words, all would have been well. Doubtless he was badly advised by his ministers. Even the able Witte believed firmly that benevolent autocracy was the best system for Russia. But the Tsar cannot be entirely excluded from blame. He was a deeply religious man who believed that his autocratic power was given to him by God, and his capacity for being obstinate at the wrong time was well-known in Court and diplomatic circles.

Be this as it may, the consequences of the day were disastrous. Not for nothing had Gorky, whose real name was Peshkov, assumed the pen-name of 'Bitter', and bitter was the reckoning for the supporters of autocracy. As a result of the shooting, even Liberals, who had set a stern face against violence, approved or at least condoned the bloody reprisals that followed.

Within less than a month of January 22 the Grand Duke Serge, uncle of the Emperor and a much haughtier and more arrogant reactionary than his nephew, was assassinated within the precincts of the Kremlin as he was driving home. The method was the same as at the assassination of the Emperor Alexander II. A young man, ready to die for his beliefs and selected for the crusade by the fighting organisation of the Socialist-Revolutionaries, threw a bomb into the Grand Duke's carriage.

More strikes followed. The professional classes organised themselves and demanded a constitution. The peasants renewed their attacks on the landowners. The numerous nationalities inside the Russian Empire—Poles, Finns, Estonians, Letts and the various races of Asiatic Russia—claimed home rule. On June 27 the cruiser *Potemkin* mutinied before Odessa, an incident which was later to form the subject of one of the Soviet Union's greatest films.

While these unpleasant events were taking place, the Russian forces in the Far East were crumbling rapidly to final defeat. Beaten on land at Mukden, the Russian armies were forced to retreat. The knock-out blow came when the Baltic Fleet was destroyed by the Japanese in the strait of Tsushima on May 27.

Yielding slightly to the rising storm of discontent, the Tsar agreed to the establishment of a Duma or Parliament. As its functions were to be only consultative, the offer, not made until August 19, was too little and too late.

Meanwhile, forced by defeat in the Far East and disorder at home, the Russian Government sued for peace. The conference took place at Portsmouth, USA, under the chairmanship of President Theodore Roosevelt. The Russian delegation was headed by Count Witte. He obtained better terms than might have been expected, and peace was signed on September 5, 1905.

It brought no relief to the internal disorders which were now reaching their zenith. Throughout the whole country the peasants were seizing the estates of the landowners and occupying their houses. The individual Russian peasant of those days was a simple, kind-hearted man, but, when he became one of a mob, he was capable of almost unbelievable savagery. More important in respect of later developments was the establishment in St Petersburg of the first Soviet or Council of Workers' Deputies. It was formed mainly as a strike committee, and its first chairman was the now almost forgotten Khrustalev-Nosar. Its vice-chairman and subsequent chairman was an active young man of nearly twenty-six. His name was Lev Davidovich Trotsky.

It was fortunate for the Tsar that at this moment Count Witte had returned from the United States, for the Government's authority was virtually at an end. Assessing the situation accurately, Count Witte, whose reputation had risen again as a result of the peace with Japan, advised the Tsar to make concessions. He was successful in obtaining from him not only the Premiership, but also the Manifesto of October 30 which conferred on the Russian people an elected legislative chamber and the promise of the customary democratic freedoms.

If the Russians had possessed any genius for compromise, they would have defeated the autocracy peacefully and gradually and established a democratic régime. But, as usual, each party, each class, each profession, wanted its all or nothing. It was not even a question of yielding, say, fifty per cent of a political programme. No one was prepared to give way to the extent of five per cent. The Constitutional Democrats, drawn from the professional classes and intelligentsia, wanted a constitutional monarchy; the Socialist-Revolutionaries wanted the land for the peasants; the Menshevik Socialists wanted a democratic Republic. Only the Octobrists, who took their name from the October Manifesto and who were composed mainly of the industrial and commercial magnates, were prepared to accept the Manifesto as it stood.

The attitude of Lenin, who was still abroad, was clear-cut. He wanted no Duma. He was even against the Soviet of Workers' Deputies when he first heard of it, but quickly changed his mind when he returned to Russia for a few months in November, 1905, and found Trotsky at the head of it. He was against elections, which he regarded as a fraud. What he wanted was an armed rising. At what was in reality the first Congress of the Bolshevik Party in London from April 25 to May 10, 1905, he had formulated this policy and from then onwards had advocated it through the whole period of trouble. Several subsequently famous Bolsheviks were present at this conference, notably Litvinov, Kamenev and Lunacharsky.

With virtually two governments operating in St Petersburg, the end of October, 1905, was the crucial moment. For a few days no one knew what would come out of the existing chaos. But the Emperor's Manifesto with its promise of a Parliament elected by the people and the complete lack of unity among anti-reactionary parties turned the scales in favour of the Government. The Manifesto widened the divisions among the parties, and cautiously but surely Count Witte began the counter-offensive. Marshalling employees and peasants still faithful to them, the landowners began to put down with great severity the widespread violence of the peasantry.

There remained the St Petersburg Soviet and the insurgent workers in the large cities. It was at this ebb in the tide of revolution that Lenin, still determined to turn the existing anarchy into an armed rising, returned to Russia. The St Petersburg Soviet continued to call for a general strike and for the summoning of a Constituent Assembly, but the response of the public was progressively feebler, and on December 16, 1905, the Government was able to arrest nearly all the members of the Soviet, including the Executive Council.

For the moment St Petersburg had had enough, and the last stand for the revolution was made in Moscow where it took the form of the armed rising on which Lenin had always insisted. Organised by the local Bolsheviks—Lenin was at that time in Finland—the insurgents, armed with rifles and protected by barricades, put up a stout resistance for ten days, but, when the Government sent a Guards regiment to Moscow, the end came quickly.

Inevitably Lenin, whose tactics had failed signally, was subjected to severe criticism, not only by the Mensheviks but also by members of his own party. He was accused of recklessness and of sacrificing the blood of the workers to prove his own theories. To some extent the criticism was justified by his own conclusion, which he maintained to the end of his life, that the attempt had been a dress rehearsal and the failure an invaluable object lesson.

With their defeat in the field of insurrection, the hopes of the Liberal and left-wing parties were now fixed on the new Duma. The elections were held in March, 1906, and, although the franchise was limited, ended in a sweeping victory for the anti-Government parties. The most successful party was the Constitutional-Democrats, known from their initials *Ka-de* as the Cadets. Out of a total of 478, they won 179 seats to which were added the sixty-three seats of the autonomous nationalists (mainly Poles) who voted with them. Next came the *Trudoviks*, or Labourites, who won ninety-four seats and claimed to speak for the peasants. Partly under the influence of Lenin, who from the beginning would have nothing to do with the Duma, all the Socialist parties abstained.

Annoyed by the electoral success of the Liberal elements, the Tsar had dismissed Witte, the one man who might have saved the dynasty and had replaced him, first by Goremykin, then by Stolypin, who had a good record as a firm administrator.

On May 10 the fundamental laws for the new Duma were announced. They came as a great disappointment to the democratic parties, for the Duma's power had been cut down to almost nothing. Foreign affairs and control of the fighting services remained in the hands of the Tsar, who also would appoint ministers. Even the legislative rights promised to the Duma had to be shared with a State Council rigged to favour the Crown. When the Duma was not sitting, the government could act by decree.

When the Duma met in May, 1906, it demanded, among numerous other reforms, an extension of its rights and the suppression of the State Council. Its ardour was impressive. In a few weeks it made 373 interpellations. The Government was not impressed and gave no answer. When the Duma made an appeal to the country, the Tsar ordered Stolypin to dissolve it.

Although he promised new elections for a second Duma in 1907, Stolypin made use of the delay to carry out a ruthless repression both in the towns and on the land. Field courts-martial were set up in all those parts of the country where the excesses had been most violent, and through the help of *agents-provocateurs* the secret police were able not only to lay their hands on many agitators, but also to acquire invaluable information of the movements and intentions of the revolutionary leaders abroad. Russian *agents-provocateurs* were recruited mainly from genuine revolutionaries who, tempted by money, betrayed their comrades. The exposure of Azev helped to demoralise the Socialist-Revolutionaries. Malinovsky, who joined the Bolsheviks, was elected to their Central Committee and even became a deputy in the Duma from 1912 to 1914. Lenin for a long time refused to believe the evidence of his treachery when it was laid before him.

All through this period of storm and stress, Stolypin was not merely an administrator. He was a reformer whose great ambition was to convert the Russian agricultural system, based on the centuries-old *mir* or commune, into individual peasant proprietorship. This innovation, introduced in the autumn of 1906, was popular, but inevitably the process was slow. It had made only small progress in relation to the size of the country when in September, 1911, he was assassinated in the theatre in Kiev by a sinister individual called Bogrov, who was simultaneously a Socialist-Revolutionary and an agent of the political police. The Tsar, who had been turned against Stolypin by the whispered calumnies of jealous members of the Court, was present at the performance.

During the period from 1906 to 1917 there were in all four Dumas. The second Duma met in March, 1907. Although the franchise had again been rigged to favour the Government, the Opposition won sixty-eight per cent of the seats. On this occasion the Socialist-Revolutionaries and the Social-Democrats of both parties participated and inevitably they took votes away from the Cadets. For a time the Duma worked better with Stolypin, and the Budget was passed. But the propaganda of the Social-Democrats caused more trouble, and after a session of three months Stolypin again dissolved the Duma.

At the next election a new electoral law favoured the Government and the Octobrists or Centre Party won the largest number of seats. The Right was also strongly represented, and, as the majority was pro-Government, the third Duma lasted nearly its full term of five years.

The fourth Duma, which met in 1912, returned a still stronger representation of the Right and gave little trouble to the Government. In less than seven years it had changed from something resembling a real Parliament to a more or less innocuous instrument of the autocracy.

From 1907 to 1912 Russia enjoyed both progress and prosperity, and even a certain relief from political upheaval. More land was given to the peasants, who in 1914 owned nearly half the land in European Russia and rented a good deal of that still in the possession of the State or large proprietors. Crop yields increased considerably. Industry continued to expand, and in 1913 Russia produced 36 million tons of coal as compared with 18 millions in 1905. The industrial proletariat had risen to two millions. Although there were still many restrictions on normal freedoms and crippling handicaps were placed on subject races like the Poles, the Finns and the Jews, the number of primary schools was largely increased with the aim of achieving compulsory universal education by 1922. Between 1907 and 1912 the expenditure on schools and the consumption of paper were doubled.

In 1912 the political calm was disturbed again when the workers of the English-owned Lena Goldfields were brutally and stupidly shot down by the gendarmerie. Another wave of strikes and minor disturbances followed, but were not very serious. Most of the leading Socialist-Revolutionaries, Mensheviks and Bolsheviks were either abroad or in Siberia. In particular, Lenin was abroad and spending his time in wrangling with the Mensheviks. At the Prague Conference of 1912 he turned his own group into an independent party and firmly rebuffed efforts by Russian and foreign socialists to heal the split. Two lessons, however, he had learnt from the revolution of 1905. One was that the proletariat could not make a successful revolution on its own. It must have the aid of the poorer peasants and, better still, of the armed soldiery. The second was that the experiment of 1905 was not a total failure. It had weakened Tsardom and could be repeated with every prospect of success.

One more date in the Revolution of 1905–6 remains to be chronicled, for it gave the revolutionaries an ally of whose very existence they were at that moment totally unaware. On October 26, 1906, Grigory Efimovich Rasputin was admitted for the first time into the presence of the Emperor and Empress.

The Emperor duly recorded the visit in his diary: 'At a quarter past six Grigory came to us. He brought an ikon of St Simeon of Verkhoturie. He saw the children and talked with us till quarter past seven.'

As Paléologue states in his *Precursors of Lenin*, in making this diary entry, the Emperor had no idea that he was writing his own sentence of death as well as that of Tsarism.

II

The War and the
March Revolution

'Yes, serfdom is abolished, but millions and millions of Russians are still without their daily bread.'—*Turgenev in 'Fathers and Sons'*.

'The opinions which our friend [Rasputin] expresses about people are, as you know, sometimes very strange. They should therefore be received with prudence.'—*Letter of the Emperor Nicholas II to the Empress*.

'I have unlimited faith in the wisdom and perspicacity of our friend, because they come from God. He sees very far into the future. His judgment should therefore be trusted.'—*Reply of the Empress to the Emperor Nicholas II*.

I

On the Eve

I ARRIVED in Moscow early in January, 1912, as a young Vice-Consul of twenty-four and, apart from two short visits to the United Kingdom in January, 1913, and in the autumn of 1917, I remained in Russia until October, 1918, when I was released from prison in the Kremlin and exchanged for Maxim Litvinov, then the Bolshevik diplomatic agent in London. I was thus for nearly seven years an eye-witness of the tumultuous events which led to the destruction of Tsarism, the collapse of the only period of democracy which Russia has ever known, and its replacement by another autocracy based on the dictatorship of the proletariat.

The Russia of 1912 was a very different country from the Russia of today. As long as one steered clear of all politics, a foreign official had as much freedom as anywhere else in the world. The contrast between wealth and poverty, however, was stark open to the eye, and in the cities there were too many human wrecks and alcoholics of the type portrayed by Gorky in his drama, *The Lower Depths*. Vodka was the cure for poverty, cold and all human unhappiness. Half-a-litre of the state red-label brand cost sixpence, and the addict, as soon as he came out of the state monopoly shop, had a knack of loosening the cork by banging the bottle just above his knee, emptying the contents in one gulp, and then falling with arms outspread into the snow.

St Petersburg, then the capital, was the city of the nobility. Moscow was the home of the rich manufacturers and merchants. Both cities had an intellectual liberal circle composed of writers, actors and artists. As is natural in a society in which twenty per cent were highly educated and the other eighty per cent totally illiterate, the book-shops were full of high-brow literature and the newspapers were serious in matter and brilliantly written. Neither in Moscow nor in St Petersburg was

45

there any newspaper even remotely resembling the yellow Press of the United Kingdom and the United States, nor were there any high-powered editors who believed that only sex, crime and money sold newspapers and therefore convinced themselves that they were giving the public what it wanted.

The aristocracy of St Petersburg had a curious form of snobbishness. In relation to other Russians the aristocrats kept to themselves. If they liked a foreigner, they made no difference between an ambassador and a commercial traveller. If the latter were really amusing, he would never be out of their houses. If the ambassador was boring, he was left alone. In Moscow money counted for more than blue blood, and with industry booming the rich were numerous. The picture which the Communists draw of the Russia of 1912 as a kind of desolate wilderness in which nothing modern existed, is deliberately inaccurate. It is almost true to say that Russia made more progress from 1884 to 1914 than between the two world wars.

The British diplomatic and consular representation in Russia was infinitesimal in comparison with the large staffs of today. The Embassy in St Petersburg consisted of an ambassador, a counsellor, five secretaries and a translator. There were also a military attaché and a naval attaché, but no typists. The expensively educated secretaries did the typing and ciphering themselves. The Embassy knew little or nothing of Russian life outside the official circles of St Petersburg, but, as all political work was concentrated in the capital and as roving about and poking one's nose into other matters were not encouraged, the staff had little or no freedom of choice.

The Consulate in Moscow consisted of one room in the Consul's house in a rather remote side-street. There was no clerical staff. I was clerk, secretary, door-keeper and typist. It was a most useful experience, for I learnt to type in Russian, and, looking back on a varied experience, I think that my first two years in Russia were the happiest in my life.

On my arrival in Moscow I had two great slices of luck. I went into a Russian family to learn the language. By sheer good fortune I was taken in by the widow of Alexander Ertel, a well-known Russian novelist and a friend of Leo Tolstoy. She and her daughter were brilliant and exacting teachers. Moreover, they were what we should call Liberals in their political sympathies, and to their flat came members of the intelligentsia, including writers and members of the theatrical profession. Among them was Michael Lykiardopoulos, a Russian of Greek descent and Secretary of the Moscow Art Theatre. Before 1914 I had met many of the leading members of the Moscow intelligentsia, and my best Russian friends were amongst them. Politically most of them were Cadets. All wanted some form of democratic Russia.

My other piece of good fortune was my meeting with Mr Harry Charnock, the managing director of the huge Vicoul Morozov textile factory at Orekhovo-Zuyevo, a purely industrial town some forty miles from Moscow. I met him on my first evening in Moscow, and, connecting vaguely the name of Bruce Lockhart with some form of football, he invited me to play for his workers' team called the Morozovtsy. I accepted at once. They were the best team in Russia then, and by playing for them I acquired a valuable insight into both Russian sport and Russian factory life.

During my first year in Moscow I had an interesting experience of the extraordinary measures taken to protect the Tsar. In 1912 the Emperor came to Moscow for the centenary of the Battle of Borodino. It was his first visit to the ancient capital and cradle of Russia since the disaster on the Khodynka Field at the time of his coronation. Before the visit the Consul and I had a tedious time with the police who required all kinds of particulars about the political reliability of British nationals living anywhere in Moscow within range of the Tsar's route. Similar and doubtless much stricter precautions were taken in regard to all Russian nationals. For the first two years of my Moscow career much of my Consular work was with the Russian Passport Department. Before the First World War Russia and Turkey were the only European countries in which passports were required. In Russia every citizen had to have a passport and, whenever he went even on a short visit to another town, he had to have his passport stamped by the police both on arrival and on departure.

At this time I was too busy learning the language and increasing my knowledge of the Russian scene to be preoccupied by Russian politics. In so far as I was interested in the international situation, I was much more afraid of a war with Germany than a revolution in Russia. In the summer of 1913 I had met General Sir Henry Wilson, who had been attending the Russian manœuvres, and he seemed quite certain that sooner or later war would be inevitable.

There was another international expert who did not believe that war was inevitable or even likely, but who hoped eagerly that it would come. This was Lenin who, in the years immediately preceding the war, was living in Cracow and was busier than ever writing books and articles, denouncing all Marxists who did not agree with his particular interpretation of Marx and praying for a war which would prepare the way for a successful revolution. It was from Cracow that in 1913 he wrote to Gorky: 'War between Austria and Russia would be very useful to the cause of the revolution in *Western* Europe. But it is hard to believe that Franz Josef and Nicholas will give us this pleasure.'

It was, too, from Cracow in February, 1913, that Lenin wrote to Gorky on another matter. 'We have here a wonderful Georgian who is writing a long article for *Prosveshchenie*' (the review *Education*). The wonderful Georgian was Stalin, who had been attending a meeting of the Bolshevik Central Committee in Cracow. Lenin had met him at the Tammerfors, Stockholm and London conferences, but it was at Cracow that he first had a really long conversation with him. On his return to Russia from Cracow Stalin was arrested, doubtless on information supplied by Malinovsky, the *agent-provocateur* who was exposed the very next year. Stalin was sent to Siberia where he spent the years of the First World War until he was released by the March Revolution of 1917.

From the beginning, 1914 remains in my memory as a year of foreboding. Russia was believed to have reorganised her army, reinforced her strategic railways on her Western front, and increased the size of the Black Sea Fleet. She had also resumed her role of protectress of the Balkan Slavs, whose victory over Turkey in the war of 1912 would have been more helpful to the Russians but for the quarrel waged between Bulgaria and Serbia over the spoils. Not even the so-called experts, however, had any firm knowledge of Russia's real strength, which depended more on national unity, national character and national efficiency than on numbers of men and expenditure on armaments.

Since the death of Stolypin and the dismissal of Kokovtsev, his successor as Prime Minister, in January, 1914, reaction was more firmly established than ever in the Government, and the workers of St Petersburg were again restive. A strike at the Putilov munitions factory in the capital ended in the usual foolish way. The police fired on the crowd, and another epidemic of strikes followed.

More serious to the régime was the fact that the sinister influence of Rasputin on the Emperor and Empress was becoming known, if not yet to the broad masses, at any rate to the educated public of St Petersburg and Moscow.

At least one film and numerous books had dealt sensationally with the life of this baleful man, who was an illiterate peasant born in Siberia. Almost everything about him was bogus. He was not a priest, but merely one of those lay brothers or pilgrims who, by growing a beard, wearing a cassock and mumbling a few prayers, used in Tsarist times to go from monastery to monastery and receive hospitality. From his youth he had been dissolute and much given to lechery and drunken orgies. His real name was Novykh, and Rasputin, the libertine, was merely a coarse peasant nickname given to him on account of his sexual prowess.

The Russian peasant of those days was a mixture of sinner and saint, repentance following rapidly after repletion and taking the place of what Anglo-Saxons call a hangover. Rasputin made his way with the Orthodox clergy by the apparent sincerity of his repentance and also by the mystic visions which he saw and was able to recount. The high Russian clergy had a special liking for lost sheep, particularly lost sheep who had dreams and the power of second sight and hypnotism.

After several years of wandering and of alternating debauchery and apparent piety, he was received by Archimandrite Theophan, the confessor of the Empress, and by Bishop Hermogen, both of whom were eager to see how great a change repentance had wrought in this no mean sinner. They were delighted with the reformed character of the penitent and much impressed by his powers of divination. Doubtless, too, they were aware that the Empress was not only deeply superstitious, but also mentally neurotic and beset by the obsession that God had ordered her to hand down to her son the absolute powers of the autocracy unimpaired. The son whom she had despaired of bearing after the birth of four daughters suffered from haemophilia. The realisation that the illness of her son came through her made the Empress an easy prey to any mystic who professed to cure him and who could confirm her belief that the Almighty was in favour of absolutism.

Rasputin was not the first thaumaturgist who had captivated or hypnotised the Empress, but he was the most successful and the most lasting. From the first day he established his ascendancy over both the Empress and Emperor, mainly because he was cunning or possibly crude enough not to alter his own rough peasant manners. Had he cringed or fawned, his influence would have waned quickly. Instead, he spoke his mind freely and firmly, using the rough speech of a peasant and warning both Emperor and Empress of the dire fate that awaited them if they disregarded his words. He was of course more absolute than the Imperial absolutists, and his success grew with the rapidity of a forest fire. He remained the chief power behind the throne until his own violent end.

The strength of his position brought to him a retinue of high-born sycophants who sought preferment through his influence. To do him justice, Rasputin in no way altered his mode of living. When he first entered the Imperial entourage in October, 1906, he was thirty-five and at the height of his physical strength. When Satan re-visited him, and the visits were regular, he liked nothing better than to steal away to some low-class *kabak* and enjoy himself with a litre of vodka and a light-o'-love, preferably a sturdy peasant girl.

In spite of the domination of Rasputin and of the spate of strikes which during the first three months of 1914 had called out nearly a million and a half workers, the incalculable Russians seemed momentarily to unite as the danger of war became clearer. In June, 1914, the First Battle Cruiser Squadron of the Royal Navy under Admiral Beatty came to St Petersburg, and a number of the officers and ratings also visited Moscow. In both cities officers and ratings received a tumultuous welcome, and British prestige rose high.

On June 28 the Archduke Franz Ferdinand was murdered, and to my surprise the Russians, who realised far more quickly than Western Europe that the assassination of the heir to the Austro-Hungarian throne meant war, took the blow calmly. Excitement rose with the Austrian ultimatum to Serbia, and sympathy with the small Slav state took the form of action. Russia mobilised thirteen of her thirty-seven army corps. On July 21 came Russia's general mobilisation which took place in excellent order. On August 1 Austria and Germany declared war, and the next day the citizens of St Petersburg and Moscow were asking why Britain was hanging back. In both cities British officials spent three anxious days during which their windows might have been smashed. August 4 came as a relief, and instead of stones we British received kisses. For days I had seen the troops marching to the railway stations and singing lustily. The vast crowds cheered them. There was no drunkenness, for the Emperor had forbidden the sale of vodka. As far as anyone could judge, the enthusiasm for the war was great, and virtually all Russia was behind it—all except one small party and one man. In St Petersburg the handful of Bolshevik members of the Duma stood aloof from the furore of patriotism, and the Bolshevik Committee issued a leaflet with the slogan: *Down with the War! War against War!* It had no effect upon the populace, now intoxicated by martial ardour and the music of war, and the Bolsheviks went underground. Lenin, who received the news of the declaration in Galicia, was having trouble with the Austrian authorities and was kept under arrest until Viktor Adler obtained his release by assuring the Austrian Minister of the Interior that here was one Russian who was a greater enemy of Russia than the minister himself.

Lenin, whose name already stood for revolution, was against the war and for the continuation of the struggle against Tsarism. His anger against those Menshevik and Bolshevik exiles who enlisted in the French Army was mild compared with his rage when he heard that the great Plekhanov had thrown his full weight behind the Socialist defenders of the war.

2

The Russian Steam-roller

ALTHOUGH General Sir Henry Wilson had told me that the French army was fully equal, if not superior, to the German army and that the Russian forces, in which I had no confidence, could be regarded merely as a little extra weight to turn the balance in favour of the Allies, the war began with collapse on the Western front and a general advance by the Russian armies on the Eastern front.

Enthusiasm was great both in Russia and in France and Britain. In the Duma all parties, except the small group of Bolsheviks, formed the *union sacrée* for the defence of the motherland. In Britain the newspapers, with more gratitude than knowledge, wrote hopefully of the Russian steam-roller.

The Russian advance bore little resemblance to anything so deliberate and mechanical as a steam-roller. It was undertaken gallantly by troops, short of heavy artillery, but strong in cavalry, in order to bring relief to the hard-pressed Anglo-French armies. Disaster, severe but far from decisive, came quickly. Through lack of proper liaison the two armies of General Samsonov and General Rennenkampf failed to unite and were defeated separately at Tannenberg and at the Masurian Lakes. Undismayed, however, the Russians continued to advance with brilliant success. I remember vividly attending in my official capacity a gala performance of Rostand's *L'Aiglon* in Moscow on September 10, 1914, to celebrate the capture of Lvov and of 100,000 prisoners by the Russian armies in Galicia. During the performance the French Consul-General received the official news of the result of the Battle of the Marne. General Joffre's telegram *'Je suis heureux de vous annoncer victoire sur tout le front'* was read out from the stage, and the audience was frenzied with delight. Strong men embraced one another, and emotion flowed over into tears as the orchestra played the two finest national hymns ever composed: *God Save the Tsar* and *La Marseillaise*. It was not yet the end of the Russian victories, but it was the last occasion on which the Russian people were united in confidence of their ability to win the war.

The autumn of 1914 brought a heavy, though not unexpected, disaster. Turkey declared war on Russia. As the German Navy controlled the Baltic Sea, this meant that the West had only the port of Archangel in summer, and in winter the tiny port of Alexandrovsk on the Murmansk coast, at which to land supplies for a Russia deficient in transport and woefully short of arms and munitions. Although it was not realised at the time, the closing of the exit from the Black Sea was really a knock-out blow.

For Russia 1915 was the critical year of the war in that it marked the gradual decline from enthusiasm to loss of hope and to the apathy which is so often the prelude to discontent and violence. The year began with another Russian offensive in East Prussia. Once again the Russians advanced too far and suffered a severe defeat at Augustovo. This disaster gave me another insight into the rapidity with which the Russians could go from one extreme to the other; in this instance, from confidence to despair. A friend in the Moscow newspaper world telephoned to tell me that the Russians were retreating to Smolensk. One of the actors of the Moscow Arts Theatre came to see me in order to tell me a piece of news from an unimpeachable source. The Germans had taken Warsaw. The source was a friend of an English journalist in St Petersburg. Neither of the stories was true. But the occasion was typical of the inability of the educated Muscovites to take a calm view of any situation. They were always either in the heights or down in the lowest depths, and Moscow was a paradise of patriotism compared with St Petersburg where the pro-German element was powerful in Court circles.

It was at the time of the Augustovo disaster that I heard of the first murmurings against the Imperial Family. It took the form of a story. The young Tsarevich, then ten years old, was found in tears by a general who was just leaving the Palace. 'What is wrong?' asked the general kindly. Half-smiling, half-crying, the Tsarevich replied: 'When the Russians get beaten, Papa cries. When the Germans are beaten, Mama cries. When am I to cry?'

Within a month of Augustovo St Petersburg and Moscow were smiling again. Good news had come from the Austrian front. On March 22 the Russians had taken Przemysl with 117,000 prisoners, and, as I was now in charge of the Consulate-General, I went to the official thanksgiving service at the Uspensky Cathedral in the Kremlin. The spring thaw had begun, and the sun shone brightly on the blue and golden cupolas of the churches and on the smiling faces of the people in the streets. By the end of April the Russian armies had penetrated into Hungary.

At this moment the war took a new turn which exposed to the world the inability of Russia to sustain a victorious campaign. The Russian armies could beat the Austrian armies, whose ranks were full of Slavs who sympathised with, and deserted to, the Russians, but Russia was no match for a highly industrialised and well-armed country like Germany. On May 2, 1915, the Germans launched their counter-offensive in the East, and gradually the whole Russian front crumbled. In June Przemysl and Lvov were recaptured, and, as the Russian armies retreated everywhere, it became known to the masses that the disasters and the retreat were caused by an almost total lack of shells and even rifle ammunition. There were competent industrialists in Russia who could have built an efficient war industry, but the autocracy had always kept everything connected with the armed forces in its own hands. As the wounded poured into the big cities, they told their relations that they had had nothing to fight with except their bayonets. The whole country, fed by rumour which travelled with the speed of the bazaar telegraph, raged against the German influences in St Petersburg.

In Moscow the populace, perhaps not entirely discouraged by Prince Yusupov, the Governor-General and a stern anti-German, spent three days in looting the numerous German shops and offices in the city and its environs. At a German factory in the proletarian district the German manager was killed, and to restore order the troops had to fire on the mob. In point of fact, the casualties were tiny, for the soldiers fired over the heads of the crowd. The damage to property, however, was enormous, and Prince Yusupov, father of Felix, who killed Rasputin, was removed from his post.

From the beginning of the war the Emperor and the Government had made no effort to call on the united effort of the nation. On the contrary, they had done their utmost to reject it. Now, however, under the pressure of defeat, the Union of Zemstvos and the Union of Cities, known together as Zemgor, were encouraged to make munitions, uniforms and numerous other articles for the war. Had these measures been taken before the war or even at its beginning Russia would not have fared so badly.

With discontent spreading through the country, the Tsar made some concessions. He dismissed two of his most unpopular ministers and, on July 9, 1915, he recalled the Duma which had met only once since the beginning of the war. It met on August 1. The *union sacrée* had not withstood the defeats in the field and the blunders of the autocracy at home, but it was still patriotic. Its main demand was for a ministry enjoying the confidence of the country. Five days after it met, Warsaw fell, and gloom descended on the whole of Russia.

Even in war the trivial is often mixed with the momentous. It was not against the Germans that the Russians vented their discontent. There were also bitter whispers about the British, especially in St Petersburg. No Russian of those days had ever expected much from the British army. But the British Navy was held in the highest respect. Russians believed it could force its way into the Baltic and the Black Sea as easily as a man knocks a cork out of a vodka bottle. Its apparent idleness could be explained in only one way. It wished Russia to be bled white. The British would fight to the last drop of Russian blood. The rumour, probably spread by pro-Germans, went round the country and was as widespread as in the Second World War.

On August 23, 1915, at one of the worst moments of the war, the rumour began to circulate through Moscow and St

Petersburg that the British Fleet had forced the Dardanelles. It was said to come from the banks, which, symptomatically enough, were regarded by Russians as more reliable than the Press or the Government. In the afternoon a Moscow evening paper brought out a special edition describing in full the fall of the Dardanelles. There were at once manifestations of joy in the main streets, and in many places people knelt on the bare stones and thanked God for the victory. The hopes so falsely raised merely increased the despondency.

With my French colleague I made a strong protest to the Prefect who told us that he had taken the severest measures possible. He had closed the newspaper for the duration of the war. I was angry, but not surprised when it came out the next afternoon in exactly the same form, but with a new name.

Among other deficiencies the food shortage began to become acute. In Moscow there were long bread queues outside the shops, and in Ivanovo-Voznesensk, a factory town, there was a demonstration against the Government and against the war. As usual, it ended with a fusillade by the soldiery. In various places, too, there was trouble over the calling up of reserves. One of the worst features of the war administration was the mobilisation of nearly 14 million men, the vast majority of whom were peasants. They disliked being taken away from the land, and, as there were no arms and no transport for them, they overcrowded the cities and became fertile subjects for revolutionary and anti-war propaganda.

Like ostriches, the Government pretended not to see these manifestations of discontent, and the censorship forbade any mention of them in the newspapers and thereby merely increased the credibility of incredible rumours.

I had excellent sources of information. I was on good terms with Prince Lvov, the President of the Zemstvos Union, and Michael Chelnokov, Mayor of Moscow and President of the Cities Union. I had friendly relations not only with the leading lights of the Moscow intelligentsia, but also with the big industrialists. I knew intimately the editors of the Moscow newspapers, and I had immediate access to the Prefect of Moscow. The two men who occupied this high post during the war were of course reactionaries devoted to the autocracy, but, as the war progressed, they never tried to conceal from me the dangers of the worsening situation. Most useful of all to me were the reports of the English managers of Russian textile factories in the smaller towns of the Moscow district. Mostly Lancashire men, they were in daily contact with the workers and had a much clearer knowledge of them than had most of the Russian intelligentsia of the cities. After the fall of Warsaw, most of the Lancashire managers predicted that the end of the war would bring a revolution, though not necessarily a successful one.

The life of an autocracy depends on many circumstances, but one condition is essential. It must have an efficient autocrat, and the tragedy of Tsarism was that Nicholas II was unfit to run a village post-office. At a moment which was critical, but did not involve complete disaster, he made no attempt to win over the still patriotic Liberals, but seemed to be bewitched. Eighteen days after the fall of Warsaw he removed the Grand Duke Nicholas from the supreme command and assumed it himself. For ten years he had felt that the Russo-Japanese War had been lost because he had not taken the field as commander-in-chief. Almost the whole nation regarded the step as fatal to Russia's prospects. The Progressive Bloc of centre parties, which came into being at this time, requested a government enjoying the confidence of the nation. The Tsar's riposte was to suspend the Duma and appoint as Prime Minister, in January, 1916, the incompetent and unfortunately named Stürmer.

These events provoked a series of meetings of the political parties demanding the recall of the Duma, and a succession of strikes by the Moscow workers. I saw the Prefect with regard to the strikes. In his view they were not serious. If repressive measures had been permitted, the trouble could have been ended in five minutes. The ministers, he said, were not energetic enough. He hoped that the Duma would be recalled, because the Progressive Bloc was 'not at all serious' and, as soon as it began to talk, it would split into quarrelling factions.

There was some truth in this last remark, but, from the

beginning, the root of all trouble was not so much the back-wardness of Russia as the fact that the Emperor was domi-nated by the Empress who, when the Tsar went to Army Headquarters, became the virtual ruler of the country. And the Empress, overwrought by religious hysteria and obsessed by the divine right of Tsars, was completely under the sway of Rasputin, who had doubtless some hypnotic power, but exerted his main influence by his bogus quality of a clair-voyant in touch with the Almighty.

Through his power over the Empress, Rasputin held in his hands the destiny of Russia. At the beginning of the war he had been absent from St Petersburg. While he was spending a summer holiday in his native Siberian village, a dissatisfied prostitute from the neighbouring town of Tobolsk had plunged a knife into his bowels, and for several weeks he lay between life and death. When the war crisis was at its height in July, 1914, he did not forget to keep in touch with the Empress, but, as he was illiterate, he found someone to write his mes-sage to the Tsar in which he prophesied victory over Germany but total loss to Russia, if she were foolish enough to go to war.

Back in Petrograd (as St Petersburg was now known) by the autumn of 1914, he extended his influence by his apparent ability to stop the occasional bleeding of the Tsarevich. The public suspected that he was against the war and, if not pro-German, at least in favour of peace at any cost, including the abandonment of France and Britain. Throughout the country the peasants regarded the Empress as a German and therefore in favour of a German victory, a theory which was certainly incorrect. But with better cause the educated Muscovites suspected Rasputin of being the advocate of a separate peace. Had they been able to study the advice given by him to the Empress, they would have been surprised by the accuracy of their surmises. He had backed and encouraged the Tsar's mistaken decision to assume supreme command. More than anyone he was responsible for the widespread belief in St Petersburg, and, later, even in Moscow, that the Germans were invincible. It was he, too, who made comparisons of the

Germans with the British, very much to the latters' disadvantage. He had a compelling voice in every appointment and, what was worse, a leading part in the dismissal of the more reliable ministers.

Almost right up to the March Revolution the Liberals and the Progressive Bloc in the Duma were quite prepared to accept a government of Tsarist ministers provided that they were men competent and honest in administrative matters and pledged to carry on the war until victory was achieved. They included men like Samarin and Shcherbatov, both of whom were aristocrats, and Dzhunkovsky, a former Governor of the Moscow Province and afterwards Assistant Minister of the Interior. All three were dismissed through the agency of Rasputin; Samarin and Dzhunkovsky for approving the removal of the drunken and uproarious lay brother from a Moscow night-club to the police station. The next morning Rasputin was released on instructions from the highest quarter, and within twenty-four hours Samarin and Dzhunkovsky received their marching orders. Samarin, highly respected by all parties and classes, was then minister in charge of church matters and presumably in the Imperial opinion should have protected Rasputin.

Rumours about this unwashed and dissolute *muzhik* travelled the length and breadth of the country and did immense harm to the Imperial Family and to the autocracy. Yet for once the truth was stranger and even worse than rumour. As Kerensky was to write later, if there had been no Rasputin, there would have been no Lenin.

3

Dilemma of the Patriots

BY the beginning of 1916 the public organisations like the War Industries Committees and the Zemgor were manufacturing munitions on a large scale, and there was no lack of shells. The Russian armies were therefore able to renew the offensive on several fronts. The Army of the Caucasus, now commanded by the Grand Duke Nicholas, won several victories against the Turks, and, taking Erzerum, pushed into Persia. Less successful was the offensive against the Germans in order to relieve the French at Verdun, and the Russian losses were again very heavy. In June General Brusilov launched an offensive in the south-west—this time in order to ease the position of the Italians, and his rapid advance raised the dwindling hopes of the civilian rear.

The success, however, was only momentary. The Russian armies were now composed of half-trained young recruits and elderly reservists. The best of the officers had been killed, and with one or two exceptions the leadership was feeble. Whenever the Russians came up against the Germans, they were outmatched both in tactics and in power of gun-fire, and, by sending a brigade or two to stiffen the Austrians, the German High Command soon checked Brusilov's advance.

In the rear confusion continued to expand into almost every sphere of daily life. To the shortages of bread and meat was added the lack of fuel, which towards the end of 1916 not only forced many factories to cease work, but also brought cold as well as hunger to the suffering masses, who now felt the economic crisis much more painfully than the political.

At the same time the Emperor, out of touch with the situation in the rear, was more than ever under the influence of the Empress, who had remained in Petrograd while he was at Headquarters at Moghilev. In these unhappy circumstances he made mistake after mistake, and the tension between

Moscow and Petrograd increased monthly, if not daily. Never perhaps in history had an autocrat such an unhappy and unlucky touch on public affairs.

So serious was the general situation in the summer of 1916 that Lord Kitchener was sent out on a special mission in the hope of his being able to impress his strong personality on the Tsar and persuade him to introduce some sorely needed military, and, possibly, political reforms. Unfortunately, the *Hampshire*, the cruiser in which Lord Kitchener travelled, was hit by a mine or torpedo, and all on board were lost. Personally, even granting that Kitchener was a strong man, I doubt if he could have altered the situation in any way or stopped the rot even momentarily. The Tsar, who had no vices and no will-power, was under the influence of a much stronger character in the person of his own wife. The Empress herself was ruled by piety and superstition, and Rasputin knew exactly how to play on both. What could the unfortunate Tsar do when the Empress supported the claim of this minister and that with such recommendations as, 'he likes and respects our holy friend'? And the Tsar, who seemed to lose what little initiative he may have had, changed his ministers with a rapidity which unbalanced the whole country and made the masses, almost as superstitious as the Empress herself, speak of the powers of darkness.

The weakness of the Tsar put a heavy strain on the patriotism of the Liberals, of whom there were still many, and the supreme difficulty of their position was described allegorically in a newspaper article by Vasily Maklakov, the brilliant Moscow jurist and orator. You are taking your mother for a drive in a high-powered car. She is sitting in front beside the chauffeur. You are in the back seat. Just as the car is about to go down a long, steep and twisting hill with a sharp turn over a river bridge at the bottom, you realise that the chauffeur has lost control. What are you to do?

That was, indeed, the dilemma. Hitting the chauffeur on the head and taking the wheel yourself was akin to revolution during the world war. It would certainly lay Russia bare and open to the Germans. It might also turn the world war into a civil war, and this was just what Lenin was advocating at this very moment.

When the war started Lenin made his way with the help of the Austrian Government from Galicia to Switzerland, where were gathered together various groups of exiles of several countries. In their attitude towards the war the Russian groups were divided. The majority of the Mensheviks under Plekhanov was anti-German and supported a defensive war against Germany. The minority under Martov and Axelrod supported the so-called Socialist internationalists who were against the war and favoured an anti-chauvinist campaign in their own countries. The Socialist Revolutionaries were also divided in the same way, Chernov's group being with the internationalists, and Avksentiev's group being pro-war. Lenin, who was contemptuous of chauvinism, democracy and, above all, pacifism, had an *idée fixe* from the beginning: to turn the imperialist war into a civil war. From this line he never really swerved, although at the First Zimmerwald Conference of anti-war European Socialist groups at the beginning of September, 1915, he proposed an appeal to all soldiers and workers engaged in the war to go on strike.

He received no support, but, obstinate as ever, he did not give way one inch and voted against the final resolution which called on the workers of Europe to fight for 'peace without indemnities and contributions', which was originally a suggestion of Trotsky.

Although the Zimmerwald Conference produced a more or less permanent group which developed into the Communist International, Lenin was a lone figure from the beginning of the war until the end of 1916. During this period he was hard put to it to pay for board and lodging. Trotsky was not yet close to him, and his nearest friend and collaborator was Zinoviev. Stalin was in Siberia where, unlike Lenin, he seems not to have put his period of exile to much use, for he produced nothing during his four years there. It was typical, too, of Lenin that, during his Swiss exile, he gave to the book of articles, which he and Zinoviev wrote then and published later, the proud title of *Against the Current*.

Swimming against the current was not a pleasant task. Most of the older Bolsheviks looked on him as an unpractical fire-eater, whose extremism in trying to persuade the Bolshevik members of the Duma to declare that the Russian proletariat longed for Russia's defeat had merely resulted in their arrest and exile in Siberia.

In April, 1916, the International Socialist Committee in Switzerland held another Conference—this time at Kienthal. Lenin had a few more supporters than at Zimmerwald, but there was no enthusiasm for his calls for violent action. He made no converts. The young Swiss Socialists regarded him as mad, and but for greater madness in higher places in Russia, mad and harmless he might have remained. In his loneliness he devoted his tireless energy to writing and in 1916 published his *Imperialism, The Highest Stage of Capitalism*. It repeated the Marxist theory that capitalist competition must always provoke war. Its main theme was that Socialism could be established only by force of arms. Disarmament and pacifism were therefore the enemies of the revolution. At this stage, apart from the secret police, a few experts and the score or two of Bolsheviks still free in Russia, his name was almost unknown to the masses in Russia. His propaganda literature, however, spread by agitators, penetrated the factories and even some of the armies at the front.

Meanwhile, as if condemned by the gods to do the wrong thing, the unfortunate Tsar seemed to have committed himself more determinedly than ever to repressive measures. In this resolve he was encouraged by the Empress who was convinced that he had a mission from God to save Russia and that only as an autocrat could he fulfil his appointed task. Her daily communications to him contained such messages as: 'Be firm, my dearest. Show them the head of a master', or, 'Dearest, remember you are the supreme ruler. Crush our enemies. Be Ivan the Terrible. Be Peter the Great.'

Another tragedy in the fate of Tsarism was the balance of power between Emperor and Empress. The initiative, nervous energy and will-power which were necessary to every autocrat were wholly lacking in the Tsar. The Empress possessed all three in abundance.

In July, 1916, came another dismissal which shook not only the Russian patriots, but also their French and British allies. Since the beginning of the war the Tsar had shown one sensible attitude. He had not made any changes at the Russian Foreign Office where Sazonov, if not a great man, was an honest and competent minister who was trusted, liked and respected both by the Russian patriots and by the British and French ambassadors. The manner of his dismissal was curious. He had been to the *Stavka* (Russian Military Headquarters) and had been delighted with his reception. As he entered his train to return to Petrograd, another train arrived bringing Stürmer, the most unpopular of all the Tsar's prime ministers. Before Sazonov reached the capital, he had been dismissed and Stürmer had taken over his functions. The hopes of the educated Russians, who knew what defeat meant, fell to the lowest ebb. The illiterate masses, who had no idea of what they were fighting for, just added a little extra hate to their already more or less open dislike of the war.

Dislike of the dismissal of Sazonov, however, was a mere passing shadow compared with the storm of indignation aroused by the Tsar's appointment of Protopopov to the all-important post of Minister of the Interior on October 1, 1916. Protopopov, who like Lenin and Kerensky was born in the Volga town of Simbirsk, had been an Octobrist member of the Duma and had been regarded for a long time as a liberal. In 1916 he had even been a member of a specially selected Russian delegation which visited Britain and France in order to see the French and British war effort. Then he had fallen under the spell of Rasputin and not only had he become a favourite of the Empress but had accepted all her reactionary political tenets. Either through ambition or mental instability he was as wax in the hand of Rasputin, who desired nothing better than to have him as Minister of the Interior, for in this way the bogus priest could exercise his influence on the gendarmerie and all other forces of repression.

The Tsar had hesitated to sanction Protopopov's appointment, but a message from the Empress stating that it was now at least four years since Protopopov had been on good terms with 'our saintly friend' soon induced the Emperor to give way.

The appointment was received with such anger and disgust by all classes that the Tsar granted temporary concessions. At the request of the Grand Dukes he recalled the Duma, which met on November 14, and ten days later he replaced the unpopular Stürmer by the scarcely less reactionary Trepov who, however, came to the Duma to affirm the loyalty of Russia to her allies and to announce that the war would continue until final victory, after which Russia would receive Constantinople as a reward.

Such declarations came too late to relieve the situation. The whole country wanted a spring-cleaning in the Imperial household, and the desire to be rid of the Rasputin scandal, of which the Protopopov appointment was part, was as strong in the State Council as in the Duma. From now on resolutions, many of them adopted by the aristocracy and forwarded to the Emperor by the various provincial marshals of nobility, demanded in polite, but firm terms the removal of Rasputin and the formation of a government enjoying public confidence.

Had the Emperor acted on this advice the dynasty might still have been saved, for the Rasputin scandal created a curious unity among people of totally opposite political views, and the cry of *La Patrie en danger* would have rallied the best elements in all classes and all political parties.

Unfortunately it was Rasputin, and not the Emperor, who paid heed to the warnings. While the poor Tsar could find nothing better to do than prorogue the Duma until January 25, 1917, Rasputin, who had always prophesied a violent death for himself, had become full of suspicion. Clairvoyant or not, he saw the Neva red with blood and predicted disaster to the Imperial Family as the direct consequence of his own death.

His forebodings were not inaccurate. Since the Tsar had ignored all requests even from his strongest supporters, conspirators took the law into their own hands. On the night of

December 30, 1916, Rasputin was killed in a private mansion in Petrograd to which he had been invited. The three leaders of the plot against him were the young Grand Duke Dmitry Pavlovich, Prince Felix Yusupov and Purishkevich, a Right-wing deputy of the Duma and a well-known reactionary.

Even in death Rasputin seemed to be invested with super-natural powers. The conspirators had planned to murder him with poisoned cakes. When they saw him eat several without ill effect, they had recourse to revolvers. Even then the shooting must have been poor, for Rasputin managed to crawl half-way up the stairs before he succumbed. As if to symbolise the inefficiency of Tsarist Russia, the plotters deposited his body in a hole in the ice on the Neva, but did not succeed in making it sink.

As soon as it was discovered, it was prepared for burial under the Empress's supervision. The coffin was borne in the presence of the Emperor, the Empress, their four daughters and the miserable Protopopov.

Less than three months later a vengeful and superstitious people, now plunged in revolution, removed the coffin from Tsarskoye Selo and, taking it into a distant forest, where a pyre of wood had been prepared, burnt it until wood and corpse were ashes.

4

The Double Revolution

THE murder of Rasputin was an act intended to save the old
régime, but its only effect was to provide the anti-war agitators
with combustible propaganda and to hasten the revolution.
Only a week before the murder Protopopov had banned the
congress of the Union of Zemtvos and Cities. The deputies of
the Union had defied him, had held their congress, and had
passed a resolution which declared that 'the Government, now
become an instrument of the dark forces, is driving Russia to
her ruin and undermining the Imperial throne. In this grave
hour in its history the country requires a government worthy
of a great people. In the decisive struggle which it is waging let
the Duma justify the expectations of the people. There is not
a day to lose.'

This document, though not published, was copied and
circulated secretly both at the front and in the rear. Three days
after the assassination of Rasputin, the Tsar re-affirmed Protopopov in his appointment as Minister of the Interior. This
double defiance of the Emperor by his subjects and of his
subjects by the Emperor was not far removed from revolution,
and the year 1917 opened with many people expecting it in the
form either of a palace revolution or of a revolt of the masses.
Despair and defeat had done their work. The nation, half-
starved and numbed with cold, was exhausted.

In this critical situation Great Britain, France and Italy
made a combined effort to revive the shattered hopes of the
Russians and to instil in them the belief that victory was not
only certain, but just round the corner. Towards the end of
January a large British, French and Italian delegation arrived
in Petrograd. Each delegation was headed by a high-ranking
minister and a senior general, and both of them were supported
by staffs of political and military experts. The leader of the
British delegation was Lord Milner who had with him as

his political advisers Lord Revelstoke and Sir George Clerk and as his military advisers General Sir Henry Wilson and five other generals.

It was one of the most imposing delegations of all times, but, in the colder light of fifty years after, one realises that it was faced with one insuperable difficulty. Whom was it to inspire and encourage? Russia was an autocracy dependent on the whim of one man. The members of the delegation were the guests of ministers appointed by the Tsar who, even during the period of the delegation's stay, made changes in his Government. Even the heads of the delegation could not suggest reforms to the Tsar. Sir George Buchanan had already tried this course with the greatest tact, but, nevertheless, had been snubbed and, later, was accused, quite unjustly, by Russian reactionaries of having encouraged a revolution. The Liberal patriots would have welcomed verbal intervention, but such action on the part of the delegation would have been rightly regarded by the Tsar and his Government as interference in their internal affairs. The only constructive work of the delegation was therefore confined to the military experts who could discuss with their Russian colleagues such problems as the synchronisation of offensives and the maintenance and exchange of supplies. Inevitably the Russian generals did their best before strangers to show themselves more patriotic and more optimistic than they perhaps were in reality.

The British delegation came to Moscow, and before their arrival the ambassador summoned me to Petrograd to see Lord Milner, prepare his programme, and interpret for him. When he arrived in Moscow, I took him to see Prince Lvov and Michael Chelnokov, the heads of the Zemstvos Union and the Cities Union, and they gave him their picture of the situation soberly, but without reservations. Moreover, they presented to him a long memorandum, the conclusion of which was that if there was no change in the attitude of the Emperor there would be a revolution within three weeks. I agreed with it.

Lord Milner had seen for himself the inefficiency of the Russians and was, I think, convinced that this view of the situation was right or, at least, very likely to prove right. Nevertheless, as he told me himself, all the Russians whom he met in Petrograd had assured him that there would be no revolution and all other members of the delegation had formed a similar opinion. In his report to the British War Cabinet he therefore accepted the majority view, although he added that he had heard other opinions which were not to be taken lightly. It was quite certain that during his visit he himself had formed a very gloomy picture of the Russian scene.

Both during and after the visit of the Western delegation rumour ran riot in Petrograd and Moscow, and there was much talk of a palace revolution, but it was never more than talk. What is certain is that some of the Grand Dukes toyed with the idea and that some of the leading generals were consulted. Brusilov, who was popular with the Liberals, is said to have replied: 'If it is a question of the Tsar or Russia, I am for Russia.' Some months previously General Alexeyev, the Chief of Staff at Headquarters, had told the Mayor of Moscow that 'the Emperor is all right; it was the b——s round him who caused all the trouble.'

As no one would act the revolution came quite adventitiously. It began quietly on March 2 when the long queue of workers waiting for bread lost patience and sacked several shops. On the next day the workers of the famous Putilov arms factory came out on strike. Other strikes followed, and for the first time in the capital since 1905 there were cries of 'Down with the Autocracy'. Neither the Government nor the masses themselves had yet realised that the strikes were anything more than local. On March 7 the Emperor went to Headquarters leaving the Empress and the children alone at Tsarskoye Selo. On March 8 the women of several Petrograd factories came out on strike in order to celebrate a so-called International Day of Women Workers. As a ball rolled along snow grows in size, so the manifestations in the streets grew larger and larger until the people began to feel their power and to become more menacing.

From his Headquarters on March 11 the Tsar dismissed Protopopov and ordered the Duma to be dissolved. This time, however, the Duma refused to withdraw and, remaining in session, demanded again a ministry enjoying the confidence of the nation. But the undirected masses in the streets were now running far ahead of the parliamentarians. As they converged from the outskirts into the centre of the city the troops sent to prevent disorders fraternised with the workers and sang the *Marseillaise* with them. Only the police remained loyal to the régime. No one else tried to defend it, least of all the Petrograd garrison, which was composed mainly of reservists.

On March 11 the crowd filled the Nevsky Prospekt, the Princes Street of Petrograd, and the police, supported by a few loyal soldiers, opened fire. Other police, posted on the roofs of houses, picked off single demonstrators in a futile attempt to check the swelling tide of triumph. By killing a few people they merely assured their own deaths. Meanwhile, the vast crowd poured itself into all the corners of autocracy, arrested frightened ministers, and released the political prisoners in the architecturally lovely but grim fortress of Peter and Paul. The crowd was in happy mood, was not vicious, and had no wish to kill anyone. It had acquired many new words which it scarcely understood: 'Long Live Liberty. Long Live Freedom of Speech' were on all lips. Everyone, too, had become *grazhdanin* or *grazhdanka* which means not comrade, but citizen or *citoyen* and *citoyenne*.

On March 12, Tsarism was dead. There were thousands of officers in Petrograd, but, although nearly all were monarchists, few had lifted a finger to save the régime, which had fallen like a house of cards before the puff of a child's breath.

Throughout the war most foreign observers had formed the opinion that Petrograd, being half-hearted about victory from the beginning, was the centre of weakness and danger and that Moscow was the centre of patriotism and strength. Yet in Moscow, where I saw the so-called February Revolution from a front seat, the course of events followed the pattern of Petrograd. The first news of the dissolution of the Duma brought crowds into the streets and, in particular, before the Town Duma (municipality) where a temporary committee was sitting to deal with the situation.

On Tuesday, March 13, the revolution in Moscow was in

full flow, and again there were great scenes in front of the Town Duma. In spite of the intense cold—the thermometer was fifteen below zero, and a cloud of steamy mist rose from the dense mass of people—the crowd was cheerful and good-humoured. Without any difficulty I made my way through the throng into the building. Inside there was chaos. Workers were encamped in most of the rooms and seemed to have assumed the upper hand. After some trouble I found Michael Chelnokov. He looked very tired, although he expressed optimism. I felt that, Liberal though he was, the revolution had gone to the Left of him and that he would no longer be Mayor of Moscow. He told me, however, that in Moscow the revolutionaries were pro-war and pro-British, and Rudnev, his successor and a Socialist-Revolutionary, assured me that this was so.

On Wednesday, March 14, the news arrived from Petrograd that the Duma had set up a Provisional Committee, that Chelnokov had been appointed Commissioner for Moscow and that Gruzinov, President of the Moscow Provincial Zemstvos and a moderate, had been nominated commander of the Moscow troops which had come over *en masse*.

In Moscow there was no fighting and not a man was killed, but the pattern of events was clear almost from the beginning. The revolution, which had been the work of masses of soldiers and workers acting for the most part spontaneously, had thrust forward two groups, who were now competing for power: the Liberals, who were constitutional monarchists, and the moderate Socialists—Socialist-Revolutionaries and Mensheviks—who were republicans and wanted the revolution to go further.

On Friday, March 16, the new Provisional Government was announced to the whole country. Headed by Prince Lvov, it contained five Moscow ministers, all of them good friends of Britain and pledged to continue the war until victory was won. In the new Government there was only one Socialist, Alexander Kerensky, who was Minister of Justice. Any early enthusiasm that I might have felt for the new Government was withered by the existence of a Soviet of Workers' and Soldiers' Deputies which had been set up in Petrograd and was now sitting in the Tauride Palace, the home of the Duma. Separate soviets of workers', soldiers' and peasants' deputies were soon to be established all over the country.

On March 15 the Emperor, who had tried to come from Army Headquarters to Tsarskoye Selo, signed the act of abdication for himself and for his son in favour of his brother, the Grand Duke Michael, who also refused the throne until the Constituent Assembly, which was to be elected, pronounced its decision. By these acts the Romanov dynasty had ceased to exist. It had ruled Russia for just over 300 years. The Empire had *de facto*, if not yet *de jure*, become a republic.

The abdication, which had been assumed from the beginning of the revolution, caused amazingly little excitement. It seems to have numbed the pathetic figure of the Emperor who longed only to return to his wife and family. Like his cousin, King George V, he kept a diary. The laconic entry for March 16 was: 'It is cold and the sun shines.'

It was, indeed, cold. The next day I attended officially a great military review in the Red Square. Thirty-three thousand troops took part in the march past, which was most impressive, for the winter sun shone brilliantly on the scene. The thermometer, however was still well under zero, and in my unpadded uniform I froze. Nevertheless, we foreign observers were relieved temporarily by the smart display of the troops. The discipline looked good, and from the point of view of the Western Allies, the discipline of the army was the main interest of the moment.

As I had to write an analysis of the revolution, I spent most of my time in the streets in order to form my impressions with my own eyes. Much of what I saw was reassuring, and even some of my anti-Socialist friends believed at the moment that something really great and enduring had taken place during these days of March, 1917. I attended—again by invitation—an immense Socialist demonstration, and the order of the crowd was quite exemplary and impressed me favourably, although from the first day of the war I had never been optimistic of a sustained Russian effort. Indeed, whenever I went to the Embassy in Petrograd, I was invariably hailed or introduced by

Lady Buchanan, the ambassador's wife, as 'the pessimistic Mr Lockhart'.

What was quite clear was the dual nature of the revolution which had happened haphazardly and had brought to the fore two powers: the patriotic Liberals and the moderate Socialists. The Bolsheviks had no part in the overthrow of Tsarism, and even their agitators had played a very minor role.

What was not quite clear was the attitude of the moderate Socialists. The Liberals were committed to the war. The moderate Socialists wanted the war to cease, but with the responsibility of power began to realise that it was not at all easy for anyone to stop the war at once. This attitude led inevitably to admission of the necessity of defensive war.

What was dangerous in the situation was the characteristic Russian swing from one extreme to the other. Where under Tsarism nearly everything was forbidden, now everything was permitted. Freedom of the spoken and written word, of assembly, of worship and atheism, overflowed overnight and, like strong drink, intoxicated those who abused it.

The enthusiasm was infectious, but, as Kliuchevsky, the greatest Russian historian, wrote, 'There is no people in Europe more capable of tremendous effort for a short space of time than the Great Russian. But there is also no people less accustomed to regular, sustained, unceasing labour than this same Great Russian.'

And I might also add there is also no people so talented in the staging of pageants and processions and in the management of great crowds.

Within a few days of the actual overthrow of Tsarism three new newspapers had appeared in Moscow: *Vpered* or *Forward*, the organ of the Mensheviks, *Trud* or *Labour*, the organ of the Socialist-Revolutionaries, and *Social-Democrat*, the mouthpiece of the Bolsheviks. The first two were not exactly rabid in favour of the war. *Social-Democrat* was from the first day anti-war, was in favour of stopping the fighting at once, and in one of its earliest numbers had a bitter article against Britain.

In my long despatch to Sir George Buchanan I gave a balanced view of all that had happened, but in my summing-up I took a line and wrote: 'It seems impossible that the struggle between the *bourgeoisie* and the proletariat can be liquidated without further bloodshed. When this clash will come no one knows, but the outlook for the war is full of foreboding.'

The revolution had been unanimous, but the dual power that emerged from it was to destroy all the high hopes of human liberty, equality and fraternity which it had engendered.

III

The Triumph of Bolshevism

'The Soviet Socialist Democracy is in no way inconsistent with the rule and dictatorship of one person.'—*Lenin, Collected Works, 1923 Edition, Vol. XVII, p. 89.*

'Lenin never regarded the Soviet Republic as an end in itself. He always looked on it as a necessary link for strengthening the revolutionary movements in the lands of the West and the East.'—*Stalin, January 26, 1924 (three days after Lenin's funeral).*

'As long as capitalism and socialism remain, we cannot live in peace. In the end one or other will triumph—a funeral requiem will be sung either over the Soviet Republic or over world capitalism.'—*Lenin, Collected Works, Vol. XVII, p. 398.*

I

The Failure of the Liberals

IF the country was unanimous in its desire to be rid of Tsarism, it was hopelessly divided in its intentions for the future. The Provisional Government, headed by Prince Georgy Lvov, was composed almost entirely of Liberals. They were men of good character and high ideals, but they all lacked experience of governing. Paul Miliukov, the Foreign Minister, would have made an excellent Foreign Secretary in an established democracy, but was too rigid for struggling with the problems left by the removal of the Tsar and his ministers. The most practical men in the new government were Alexander Guchkov and Alexander Konovalov, both of whom had experience of big business and industry. Alexander Kerensky, the Minister of Justice, and the only Socialist in the Cabinet, was the link between the Provisional Government and the Soviet of Petrograd.

In its attitude towards its numerous perplexities the Government was a mixture of stubbornness and weakness. In regard to foreign affairs it was legalistic, regarded the Tsarist alliances as binding, and assured France and Great Britain of its determination to carry on the war until final victory. In internal affairs it sought to put its life-long ideals into force, and one of its first acts was to proclaim freedom of the written and spoken word, freedom of association and freedom to strike. The confusion that followed was as if Aeolus had unloosed from his sack all the winds of the world at once. Every street corner and square in Petrograd and Moscow was like a speaker's stand in Hyde Park at which budding orators harangued as many listeners as they could attract. Then was born the passion of the Russian Communist for interminable speeches.

Parallel with the Provisional Government was the Petrograd Soviet which, by installing itself in the Tauride Palace, the former building of the Duma, had not only established a topographical superiority for itself, but had also converted the

Soviet into a kind of Parliament acting as both critic and controller of the Government. In those early days it was not actively hostile, for its members were almost entirely Socialist-Revolutionaries and Mensheviks. Most of them were pleasant, humane men and women with lofty ideals. Unfortunately, they represented many different elements, had no experience of administration and, like nearly everyone in Russia, would rather have died for their principles than compromise. The president of the Petrograd Soviet was Chkheidze, a Georgian, and the most brilliant member was another Georgian called Tseretelli. The Georgians, not unnaturally, thought first of democracy for Georgia. The Socialist-Revolutionaries wanted the land for the peasants. The Social-Democrats wished to nationalise the factories. At this stage the Bolsheviks played virtually no part. They were a tiny minority in the Petrograd Soviet and their supporters in the country did not amount to more than 50,000.

In broad terms the Provisional Government was composed of *bourgeois* and was prepared to carry on the war. The Soviet was composed mainly of workers and soldiers and wanted peace, but was not prepared to leave the Western Allies in the lurch. It wanted a general peace. In the circumstances the struggle between the Provisional Government and the Soviet was more prolonged than violent. Its worst effects were to postpone and, indeed, to prevent all action and to undermine discipline both in the armed forces and in the people. Disturbing, too, was the practice of the Soviet in sending out its own propaganda and its own resolutions and in issuing orders under its own name. In this respect the notorious *Prikaz* No. 1 did great damage to discipline in the army. This order, originally intended for the Petrograd garrison, called on the lower ranks to form a soviet in each battalion and regiment, to take control of all the arms in each unit, and to cease saluting officers except when on duty. A final instruction to obey the orders of the Government was nullified by the clause 'unless they contradict those issued by the Soviet'. The news of this order travelled through the regiments at the front with the speed of a forest fire in a dry summer and, being attractive to them, was accepted and acted on immediately.

Many writers have attributed the collapse of the Russian armies to this order, but in retrospect I think it doubtful if discipline could have been maintained for long even if *Prikaz* No. 1 had never been issued. In an autocracy everything descended downwards from the ruler. With the abdication of the Tsar all the allegiances of the armed forces from the generals to the youngest private were broken, and, even before the abdication, the armies, composed of raw recruits and middle-aged reservists, had lost not only most of their fighting spirit, but also much of their interest in a war which many of the lower ranks had never understood. Few of the reservists wanted Constantinople or even knew where it was. What use was there in urging an anti-war soldier to fight because German troops were still occupying, say, the Volhynia province when the soldier answered: 'What is the Volhynia province to me? I come from the Saratov province', which was hundreds of miles behind the front.

Among the measures more or less forced by the Petrograd Soviet on the Government was the arrest of the Emperor and Empress. After signing the abdication at Pskov the Emperor had returned to Army Headquarters at Moghilev. Now on March 21 he was brought back to Tsarskoye Selo where with the Empress and his five children he was put under guard. Before leaving Moghilev he took leave of his armies in a noble and generous message which ended with the words: 'I have the firm conviction that the boundless love which you have for our beautiful country is not extinguished in your hearts. May God bless you and may St George, the great martyr, lead you to victory.'

Apart from its inability to act, the Provisional Government was faced with three great difficulties. The first was the opposition encountered from conservative elements in the privileged classes. These men now generally recognised that the old régime had had its faults, but they feared that any change would be for the worse and that the Russia they loved would be entirely disrupted. In their eyes democracy was simply chaos and anarchy. They were particularly alarmed by the upsurge of mass violence in the towns and in the countryside, which threatened their property rights, and by the apparent collapse of all established authorities. They condemned the Provisional Government for what seemed to them its weakness in dealing with 'subversion', not realising that in a fluid revolutionary situation concessions had to be made to the popular mood. Many conservatives looked to the army command to restore 'firm rule'—and ultimately, perhaps, the monarchy. The Government thus faced enemies on the Right and the Left, and had to steer a compromise course between them.

The second difficulty arose from the fact that the seat of the Government was in Petrograd, which from the beginning of the war had been regarded by the patriotic elements as the evil spirit of subversion, ineptitude and cowardice. It had sheltered all that was worst in Russia, from the gilded youth of the aristocracy and of the *bourgeoisie*, who had dodged going to the front, to the pro-German elements in the bureaucracy and to the factory workers who had been much more deeply indoctrinated with revolutionary fervour than the Moscow workers. In the eyes of the Socialists Petrograd was the city of the revolution and its heroes were the undisciplined garrison of the city. Symptomatic of the prevailing atmosphere was the amazing fact that the Petrograd Soviet had given a solemn promise to the Petrograd garrison that, as a reward for its revolutionary services, it would not be sent to the front until the war was over. Thus, in addition to the dual power of the Petrograd Soviet, the Government was sorely hampered, especially in its efforts to restore discipline, by the cramping presence of a thoroughly unreliable and rapacious soldiery. The troops' morale was a thousand times better at the front, as nearly everyone who had been there testified.

By far the greatest difficulty, however, was that of maintaining the nation's war effort. The needs of the army had to be given priority in the allocation of scarce resources, and thus the cities went short. The lack of consumer goods, and especially of food and fuel, was especially acute in Petrograd, which was a long way from the relatively better-supplied south, with its big grain farms and metallurgical works. The transport system functioned badly and many locomotives and goods waggons were out of order. Bread rationing was introduced in Petrograd on April 6. Owing to the shortage of goods prices rose, and so too did pressure for wage increases. The Government received less revenue in taxation at a time when its expenditure on the war was rapidly rising. It desperately tried to bridge the gap by increasing the amount of paper money in circulation, but this only made inflation even worse. The general price level in 1917 was three and a half times higher than in 1916. Wage-earners made exorbitant demands upon their employers and frequently ceased work or interfered arbitrarily in the working of their factories. This behaviour, together with the lack of fuel and raw materials, hastened the decline of industrial output. Within a few months managers were either closing down their factories in disgust or appealing to the Government to take them over. The authorities did what they could to reconcile capital and labour, but old hatreds and suspicions ran too deep to be bridged.

Outwardly, at least, life in Moscow had not changed very much. The old provincial governors had been superseded by commissioners, and the police, the one force which had remained loyal to Tsarism, had been replaced by a so-called militia. Soon, however, I noticed quite a number of my old constable friends among the new formation. My friend Michael Chelnokov, who had been Mayor and then Commissioner of the Moscow Province, had lost both his jobs, not because he was a reactionary, but because he had principles which he could not adapt to the new circumstances.

He was pessimistic and told me prophetically that Prince Lvov's reign would be little longer than his own. I felt sorry for him, for he had served the Allied cause nobly. As for Prince Lvov, he was a Liberal of saintly and exemplary character, a good organiser, and a genuine reformer who believed that example was better than precept. I had known him throughout the war and saw him several times in Petrograd when he was Prime Minister. He was a tired and lonely man living in two small rooms. Much as I admired him, I realised that his virtues were more suited to a missionary meeting than to a rough-house.

In Moscow the Soviet had early on divided itself into two component parts: the Soviet of Workers' Deputies and the Soviet of Soldiers' Deputies. The president of the latter, a sergeant called Urnov, was a stolid, serious man who tried to work out his problems as honestly as he could. He wanted peace, but was unwilling to 'let down' the Allies and was certainly not prepared to allow the Germans to annex any Russian territory. Poland and the Baltic provinces were quite another matter. They were entitled to freedom. But if the Germans tried to advance farther, the Russian Army would oppose them. He was in favour of a defensive war if a reasonable peace were impossible. On the whole this was the attitude of Moscow up to April, 1917.

Although virtually all Russians were tired of the war, the real defeatism was in Petrograd. While Miliukov wanted war until ultimate victory, the liberation of the minority states in Austria-Hungary, and the reward of Constantinople for Russia herself, the Petrograd Soviet had quite other ideas. Its slogan was war 'without annexations and contributions' and it had lost no time in sending out to all the belligerents—and by 1917 they were numerous—an appeal calling on them to end the war. At the same time it maintained a constant pressure on the Government to declare its war aims. The effect of this pressure was to force Miliukov to modify his first declaration.

Meanwhile, the unfortunate Foreign Minister was being harassed politely, but insistently, from a very different quarter. On instructions from London and Paris the British and French ambassadors also sought from Miliukov a fresh declaration of Russia's war aims, and by this they meant a re-affirmation of the new Russia's loyalty to the pledges given to France and Great Britain by the Tsarist government that all three countries should fight on until the enemy was defeated.

In Great Britain Lloyd George and many of the British Left-wing politicians and workers hailed the February Revolution not only as a great progressive step, but also as a valuable aid to victory. The Left-wing politicians and workers may have believed this, but Lloyd George, who doubtless desired to encourage the new Russian Government, can hardly have been deceived into thinking that the new Russia, exhausted economically and wasted physically by her enormous casualties, would spring to arms again to fight with the courage and fervour of the first armies of the French Revolution.

The French Government was more incisive. France had borne the brunt of the first two-and-a-half years of the war. Her own casualties had been crippling. She was now fighting for her existence. She had lent Russia milliards of francs in loans. Sentiment and the need of the moment over-ruled foresight. She was determined not to let Russia slip out of the war if she could possibly help it. The British attitude was perhaps not very different, but was expressed less forcibly.

Faced with the task of placating both the Allies and the Soviet, the unfortunate Miliukov fell between two stools. Having staved off the Soviet with the assurance that Russia had no intention of increasing her power abroad at the expense of other nations, she had informed the British and French Governments in writing that Russia held herself bound by all the agreements which she had concluded with the Allies. These agreements, of course, included Constantinople and the control of the entrance to the Black Sea as Russia's share of the spoils of victory.

As open diplomacy was now more or less the order of the day, because secrecy no longer could be maintained, Miliukov's Note was published on May 1. To the Petrograd Soviet its contents were imperialism at its worst and revealed Miliukov as a double-dealer. At once crowds gathered and, supported by some of the Petrograd garrison, marched towards the Marinsky Palace, which was now the seat of the Government, and demanded the resignation of Miliukov. The demonstrations lasted for two days, and there was some fighting between Bolsheviks and anti-Bolsheviks. In the procession of the workers, banners were carried bearing the slogans: Publish the Secret Treaties! Down with the War! All Power to the Soviets!

It was the first occasion on which the Bolsheviks had played a part in a big anti-war demonstration. The reason for this was not far to seek. The leading Bolsheviks, who had been abroad or in exile in Siberia, were now hastening back to the capital, for a Provisional Government, which had sanctioned all the freedoms and had released all political prisoners, could not refuse entry even to the men who, they must have realised, were more dangerous to them than the Germans. Stalin, who had been under restraint in Siberia for nearly five years, was the first back on March 25 and took over the editorship of *Pravda* from Molotov. With him came Kamenev and Sverdlov. Lenin arrived in Petrograd on April 16 and was welcomed at the Finland station by the leaders of the Soviet including Chkheidze, the Menshevik President. As the French and British Governments had refused to help Lenin to return to Russia, he accepted the offer of the Germans to send him back in a sealed railway carriage. The most recent evidence would seem to indicate that he also received some financial help from the Germans. This does not mean that Lenin was a German agent, although the manner of his arrival raised an uproar at the time. His attitude regarding his return never changed. If the Germans were such fools as to send him back to Russia, the better it was for him and the worse for them.

Before he reached Petrograd, Stalin and Kamenev had been, from the Bolshevik point of view, rather feeble in their attitude towards the Provisional Government, promising to support it in so far as it was revolutionary and to oppose it if it showed any sign of counter-revolutionary methods.

Lenin assessed the situation rapidly. The Provisional Government must go. With the Soviet in power there was no place for a parliamentary republic. The war must be stopped. The land must be taken over at once by peasant committees. The Bolsheviks' break with the Mensheviks must be complete. Realising that his following in the Soviet and in the country was small, he retired to the former palace of the famous ballerina, Kshesinskaya, to prepare the propaganda campaign which was to multiply his supporters.

Meanwhile, the governmental crisis was settled by a compromise between the Provisional Government and the Soviet majority. The basis of it was an increase in the Socialist representation and the sacrifice, first, of Guchkov, the energetic Minister of War, and a few days later of Miliukov, who was replaced as Foreign Minister by Mikhail Tereshchenko, another Liberal and then reputed to be the richest man in Russia. After the Bolshevik revolution he made a successful new career as a financier in England. Guchkov resigned mainly because he considered that democratisation of the army had gone too far and was threatening 'the defence, freedom and even the existence of Russia'. Five Socialists joined the Government, the two most important being Viktor Chernov, the leader of the Socialist-Revolutionaries, and the former Georgian deputy and prominent Menshevik, Tseretelli. The most important change, however, was the promotion of Alexander Kerensky, the man of the hour, from Minister of Justice to Minister of War.

The Government changes were announced on May 18; the previous day another revolutionary exile who was to influence mightily the destiny of Russia, had arrived in Petrograd. He was Lev Davidovich Trotsky. His real name was Bronstein.

2

Kerensky at the Helm

THE reconstructed Provisional Government lasted from May 18 to July 5. Although Prince Lvov remained as Prime Minister, the brief reign of the Liberals had really ended with the departure of Guchkov and Miliukov. The strong man of the Government was Kerensky, and from now until the next ministerial crisis in July there was a great battle of personalities and policies, with Kerensky and the moderate Socialists on the side of democracy and liberty and Lenin and Trotsky in favour of violence and dictatorship of the proletariat. The Soviet now gave general support to the coalition Government, but found itself under strong pressure from its Left wing and the Bolsheviks.

Lenin had returned to Russia one week before his forty-seventh birthday. Trotsky, dark, short and broad-shouldered with eyes that seemed to glow with energy, was thirty-nine. Kerensky, a former member of the Duma and a brilliant lawyer, was only thirty-six. Lenin, whose self-control and self-confidence were remarkable, was the brains of Bolshevism. In his long years of exile he had worked out his own idea of the tactics and strategy of revolution and had satisfied himself that they were infallible. In this respect he was completely ruthless and listened to no one. He was not a great orator in the classical sense, but on big occasions he possessed the art of convincing his audience that he was right.

Trotsky, temperamental and more like a composer in appearance than a general, had two valuable qualities: great physical courage and admirable administrative ability. When he was in the mood, he was a master of invective and could make his victim squirm, especially when he had the audience on his side. He had never joined the Bolshevik Party and had criticised Lenin strongly in the past, but with the revolution already in being he became a member of what Lenin had now christened the Communist Party. If Lenin was the planner of the Bolshevik revolution, Trotsky was the organiser.

Kerensky, whom I have known intimately for many years since 1917, had courage and persuasiveness. He had won his spurs as a lawyer by defending in the courts political opponents of Tsarism. He was outstandingly the best orator of the three and could draw momentary tears from even the stony-hearted. He was a kind and, above all, a humane man with a deep sense of decency, but, as Mr A. J. P. Taylor was to write later of Jan Masaryk, 'decency is not enough against Communism'.

Kerensky was for continuing the war, holding the view that, as the revolution had been mainly to stop a Tsarist separate peace, liberty and democracy could be established on a solid foundation only in the event of a successful conclusion to the war.

Lenin and Trotsky wanted to turn what they called the imperialist war into a civil war and from the beginning were determined to destroy the Provisional Government and to capture the Soviets all over the country. They denounced all the other Socialist parties and leaders who supported the Government as henchmen of the 'imperialist bourgeoisie' and traitors to the popular cause, and declared confidently that they would soon be overthrown in a new revolution, which would set up a 'Republic of Soviets'. It was not clear to all their listeners, most of whom were unsophisticated in political matters, that under a Soviet régime as Lenin and Trotsky envisaged it real power would in fact rest with the Bolshevik Party.

As, after the first emotional energy engendered by the overthrow of Tsarism, the Russians were exhausted and war-weary, the odds looked and were heavy against Kerensky. For a time, however, he held his own, partly because, unlike many of the Liberals, he did not under-estimate Lenin and partly because of Lenin's own mistakes. The acceptance of help from the Germans and the journey through Germany told heavily against Lenin for some weeks after his return. Serious, too, were the revelations about his friend, Malinovsky. The revolution had thrown open the archives of the Tsarist secret police, and there in black and white was the evidence that for many years Malinovsky had been in the pay of the *Okhrana* and in the capacity of *agent-provocateur* had sent many Bolsheviks including Stalin to prison or to Siberia. Long before the war Lenin had been warned more than once against Malinovsky, but indifferent, as usual, to the opinions of others and relying solely on his own judgment, he defended Malinovsky obstinately until even he could not refute the proofs in writing.

The first clash between Lenin and Kerensky, the two protagonists in the next act of the revolutionary drama, took place at the first all-Russian Congress of Soviets which was held in Petrograd from June 16, 1917, to July 7. The intensified propaganda put out by Lenin since his return had increased the number of Bolshevik supporters, but at the Congress they had only 105 delegates against 285 delegates of the Socialist-Revolutionaries and the 248 Mensheviks. In the Socialist Soviet the majority against the Bolsheviks was still more than five to one.

The oratorical duel took place on June 17, and Lenin, who was never afraid to attack, spoke first. Denouncing the war and the dangers of counter-revolution, he declared: 'The time for a break in the entire history of the Russian Revolution has come. . . . To go ahead or to retreat? This is the question. In times of revolution it is impossible to remain in one place.'

Kerensky's reply was prophetic in more ways than one. Drawing a parallel with the French Revolution, which had ended in dictatorship, he exclaimed: 'The problem of the Russian Socialist parties and of Russian democracy is to prevent such an end as there was in France—to hold on to the revolutionary conquests already made, to see to it that our comrades who have been released from prison do not return there; that Comrade Lenin, who has been abroad, may have the opportunity to speak here again, and not be obliged to flee back to Switzerland.' He accused the Bolsheviks of collaborating with the reactionaries to destroy democracy. 'When you, in alliance with reaction, shall destroy our power, then you will have a real dictatorship.'

The majority of the Congress was on Kerensky's side. But the soldiers who were present and who for the most part belonged to the Petrograd garrison, made a noisy demonstration in favour of Lenin's speech. In this connection Lenin erred once again. Mistaking noise for numbers, he made a premature attempt to overthrow the Provisional Government and summoned the workers of Petrograd to demonstrate on June 23 against what the Bolshevik posters called 'the counter-revolution'. The real object of the proposed demonstrations, however, was to undermine not only the Provisional Government, but also the anti-Bolshevik majority in the Soviets. The Congress was still sitting, and for once the majority showed some energy in action. After visiting their own supporters in the factories and assuring themselves of military support, they warned the Bolsheviks that, unless they cancelled the demonstration, the sternest measures would be taken to prevent the demonstrators from assembling. The Bolsheviks gave way, but there was no reconciliation. Lenin, the man of no compromise, withdrew only to gain more strength.

Meanwhile, as Minister of War, Kerensky had been spending most of his time at the front. The French and British Governments, who favoured the Liberals and disliked the Soviets, were eager to keep Russia in the war. With this end in view they brought considerable persuasion to bear on Kerensky. In April they had sent delegations of British and French Socialists to encourage the Soviets to continue the war and not to endanger a Socialist future by facilitating a German victory. The British delegation, composed mainly of stolid trade unionists, was neither intellectually imposing nor politically successful. The French trio were intellectuals and therefore better adapted to argue with the Marxists in the Soviet. The most patriotic Frenchman and the fiercest critic of the Bolsheviks was Marcel Cachin, who later became the chairman of the French Communist Party!

Hard on the heels of the trade unionists came Mr Arthur Henderson, the only Labour minister in the British Government. He brought with him to Petrograd Lloyd George's promise of the post of British ambassador. As this promise had been made known to the Embassy, it caused some commotion. I was brought up to Petrograd to see Mr Henderson and to arrange his programme. I took him to a full meeting of the Moscow Soviet and interpreted for him. The ordeal was severe, and long before it was over Mr Henderson had abandoned any ambition of succeeding Sir George Buchanan as His Majesty's ambassador. Personal acquaintance with the Petrograd and Moscow Soviets had horrified him. The combined impression of these Anglo-French delegations on the war and on the Russian Socialists can be compared to a drop of fresh water in the saltiest of seas.

What was perhaps unfortunate was the fact that, as Minister of War, Kerensky was under great pressure from the Allied military missions who, not unnaturally perhaps, wished to see discipline restored in the Russian army by the same methods as in other armies. At the same time the British and French Governments turned a deaf ear to Kerensky's pleading for a revision of war aims. They have their share of responsibility for the triumph of Bolshevism.

Handicapped by this Anglo-French rigidity and by the reaction in Russia itself, which had grown stronger as a result of Lenin's violent policy, Kerensky did his utmost to support the authority of the officers, and he himself spent much time at the front encouraging the soldiers. If there could have been 200 Kerenskys in front of 200 battalions simultaneously, a Russian offensive might have been irresistible, for he was a great orator. Not very long after he became Minister of War, I heard him make one of his pro-war speeches in the Bolshoy Theatre in Moscow. It was crowded with rich and poor, and the semi-circle of boxes was filled with the wealthy mercantile élite of Moscow. Kerensky's theme was on human suffering and human courage. All that was worth having in the world, from the physical pain of childbirth to the spiritual sorrow of the loss of a loved one, came through suffering, which alone tested character. He had been to the front. He had seen the soldiers who had nothing, but whose spirit was far better than that of the rear. All the grumbling and apathy came from the citizens of Petrograd and Moscow. They said that they were tired. What had they done to be tired? Could they not watch a little longer? Was he to go back to tell the men in the trenches that 'the heart of Russia' was exhausted?

He looked dead tired himself as he sank back into a chair. He was then suffering from serious kidney trouble, but he had stirred the audience to a frenzy of emotion. A rich woman threw her pearl necklace on the stage. Others did the same, and strong men wept like children. It was an amazing, but ephemeral performance.

At the request of the hard-pressed Allies, who in March and April, 1917, had been shaken by the defeat of General Nivelle's army at Chemin des Dames, Kerensky launched a big offensive which he hoped would bring him success and give him the control and support of the army. Neither he nor Lenin had any real illusions about the workers. The victor in the struggle for the leadership of Russia would be the man who had the soldiers on his side.

The offensive began on July 1, on the Galician front, and was directed towards Lvov. It was under the supreme command of Brusilov, the most popular and hitherto the most fortunate of the Russian generals, and was supported by the Central Executive Committee of the Soviets. The initial attacks were successful, and the Russian armies advanced nearly seventy miles and took several thousand Austrian prisoners. The effort, however, was short-lived. The Germans counter-attacked on July 18 and broke the Russian front at Tarnopol on July 20.

It was the end of any serious fighting by the Russians against the Germans. From now on the situation at the front became more and more chaotic. Encouraged by the Leninist propaganda to fraternise with the enemy and 'to make peace with their legs', the soldiers began to lose rapidly the slight discipline and morale that remained to them. In explaining the collapse of the front General Brusilov had reported that even before the offensive there were regiments which accepted no other authority than that of Lenin. Desertions, which had begun on a small scale from the first days of the revolution, became a daily occurrence, but had not yet assumed the dimensions of a mass movement.

There are two curious comments to be made on the offensive. First, some of the Bolshevik propaganda, including Lenin's articles, which reached the Russian front was disseminated by the Germans who, either with or without the connivance of Lenin, were able to buy the Bolshevik newspapers in Stockholm and reproduce them. Secondly, although the offensive failed, credit must be given to the Russian armies and to Kerensky for holding so many German battalions on the Eastern front. On July 1, 1917, the day of the opening of the offensive, there were the same number of German divisions on the Russo-German front as on the opening day of the March Revolution. During the July offensive the Germans increased their divisions.

Meanwhile, troubles and threats had been engaging the attention of the Provisional Government in Petrograd. The July offensive had not been popular with the Petrograd garrison and still less with the ratings of the Russian Navy. Stationed at Kronstadt, they contained the most savage elements thrown up by the Revolution. Since May 18, the day on which the Liberal-Socialist coalition had assumed office, the Liberals had lost influence inside the Government itself; the Petrograd Soviet had become more Bolshevik, and throughout the country the Bolsheviks had increased their supporters, mainly because of their anti-war propaganda.

The failure of the offensive encouraged the Bolshevik Central Committee to consider another attempt to seize power, and, although it hesitated and cancelled its original orders for a rising, a vast crowd of soldiers and workers demonstrated in the streets on July 16. On the next day the demonstrators were joined by the Kronstadt ratings who arrived in Petrograd and marched to the Bolshevik headquarters in the Kshesinskaya Palace. Here they were harangued by Lenin who had come back to Petrograd as soon as he heard of the commotion. Lenin, however, did not call for the overthrow of the Provisional Government but contented himself with denouncing the Liberals as counter-revolutionaries and the Socialists as traitors, and after a display of ugly temper before the Tauride Palace the sailors went home.

The Provisional Government took strong action. The troops faithful to the Government disarmed the Kronstadt ratings. On the appeal of the Menshevik leaders in the Soviet, the workers went home. Two days later the Government tried to arrest Lenin, Kollontay, Kamenev and Zinoviev. After hiding for some days in a house in Petrograd, Lenin and Zinoviev escaped to Finland. Both were disguised. Lenin, having shaved off his beard, assumed a wig to hide his baldness and the swarthy Zinoviev cut his long hair short. The Soviet leaders, though supporting Kerensky, were powerful enough to prevent any punishment of Trotsky who in fierce articles had provoked his arrest. Outwardly, this seemed to indicate a victory for the Government and the moderate Socialists in their struggle with the Bolsheviks, whose leaders had been forced back underground and their press organs banned. The Government published evidence to show that the Bolsheviks were in contact with the Germans, which helped to discredit them in the eyes of patriotic opinion.

But the effects of this action were short-lived, since the Government was itself in a state of crisis. Four Cadet (Liberal) ministers had already resigned on July 15, nominally because the Government had recognised the *Rada* or Council of an autonomous Ukraine, and on July 20 Prince Lvov, a man of noble character and all the virtues of a Minister except decision and capacity for action, resigned. During the months that he had been Premier the Provisional Government had shown a perhaps understandable unwillingness to force matters or to obey the rather inconsiderate exhortations of the Allied Governments to restore order. But, from the point of view of its own self-preservation, it had failed badly in two respects. It had taken no firm decision on the partition of the land and therefore was losing the support of the peasants. It had not fixed a date for the Constituent Assembly, which every worker and peasant wanted even if they had only the vaguest idea of what it meant.

After tense negotiations with the Soviet Executive Committee Kerensky became head of a new Government which, when finally constituted on August 6, included still more

Socialists and was more than ever under the control of the non-Bolshevik Socialists in the Petrograd Soviet.

The dual power which had existed from the first had strangled all decision, for, while the Soviet refused to govern, it would not allow the Provisional Ministers to do so. In a period when days were equal to months, valuable and irretrievable time was lost in a spate of repetitious speechifying. It was difficult to believe that such a situation could last.

3

The Kornilov Episode

UNDER the leadership of Kerensky the Provisional Government entered its second reconstruction and the third period of its existence. The first period had lasted from March 15 to May 15. The second period, which was marked by the entry of more Socialists into the Government, lasted from May 18 until August 6. The third period lasted until November 7. Each period saw its authority weakened, until it collapsed before the Bolsheviks almost without a fight. Kerensky remained Prime Minister until the Bolshevik takeover, but the composition of his Government changed frequently in response to the pressures exerted upon it by the party leaders. For a month (September 8–October 7) there was no regular cabinet at all, and power was exercised by Kerensky personally with the aid of a five-man 'directory'.

The period began with a display of strength by Kerensky. At last he gave an order forbidding any transaction in land until after the elections for the Constituent Assembly, which in June had been fixed for September 17, but on August 9 were postponed until November 12. It was a temporarily helpful measure, but it came too late to prevent excesses by the peasants. His most important task was to restore discipline in the Russian army. He had already appointed political Commissars to assist the High Command, and Boris Savinkov, as Commissar on the South-Western front, had contributed largely to the initial successes of the July offensive. To check desertions, Kerensky now restored the death penalty for courts-martial at the front, and his decision was more or less approved by the Executive Committee of the Petrograd Soviet. Previously he had appointed General Kornilov as Commander-in-Chief, first, of the South-Western front and, almost immediately afterwards, of all Russian forces. General Brusilov and General Gutor, who were held responsible for the failure of the July offensive, had been relieved of their posts.

General Kornilov, though small in stature with a beard and moustache which gave him some resemblance to the Tsar, was a giant in courage and a first-class commander in the field with all the virtues and limitations which the epithet implies. He was a stern disciplinarian who looked after his men well and was worshipped by them. During the war he had excelled himself as leader of the Eighth Army and had extricated it cleverly from several uncomfortable and dangerous situations. In so far as he was a politician, he was a reactionary. Later, General Brusilov was to describe him as 'a man with the heart of a lion and the brains of a lamb'.

Kornilov, however, was undoubtedly the general who had the best chance of infusing some discipline into the broken Russian armies. He had been recommended to Kerensky by Savinkov. On one subject—and on one only—the three men were agreed. The army must be disciplined and cleansed from Bolshevism. Doubtless, Bolshevism would have triumphed in any circumstances, for the counter-measures were taken too late. But the deal with Kornilov and Savinkov was to hasten the fall of Kerensky and the triumph of Lenin.

Although the 'July Days' had been another set-back to the Bolsheviks, Kerensky's position was weak and growing weaker. He had against him the Right which now comprised not only the Tsarists, but also many *bourgeois* who had been terrified by the course taken by the revolution. He was assailed daily by the extreme Left represented by the Bolsheviks who could now count on much larger support, especially in the factories of Petrograd and Moscow. He himself stood in the middle, and in Russia the middle has always been squeezed by the extremes. It was, too, a very wobbly middle which ranged from wordy, but futile, Mensheviks to less loquacious, but equally futile, Liberals.

Even before he had announced the reconstruction of his Government he had suffered a set-back at the hands of the Soviet. Making some quite innocent correspondence of the Tsar's an excuse for accusing him of plotting, the Soviet demanded the removal of the Imperial Family from Tsarskoye Selo. Influenced perhaps by the possible danger to the Imperial Family on account of its proximity to Petrograd, Kerensky gave way, and on August 1 the Emperor and Empress with their five children were removed to Tobolsk, the home town of Rasputin. Fate seemed to be against the Tsar from the first days of his reign. After the abdication there were two chances of getting him and his family out of the country. On one occasion the family had measles and could not be moved. On the other occasion Lloyd George made some temporary difficulties.

Although the collapse of the July offensive brought Kerensky to the Premiership it weakened both his personal prestige and his chances of success. The indispensable man, who was to save Russia from chaos and turn defeat into victory, had failed, as he was bound to fail, and with failure the degeneration of the whole country gained alarming speed. The subject nations began to break away, with the exception of Poland which was still under German occupation. The *bourgeoisie*, which had at one time regarded Kerensky almost as a worker of miracles, were now looking for salvation to the Cossacks. In the Petrograd Soviet the Socialist-Revolutionaries and Mensheviks had never been more than luke warm in their support of the Provisional Government and were now losing ground to the Bolsheviks. Moreover, the Soviet was full of intellectuals, who had a far higher standard of international culture than, say, the British House of Commons, but only a hundredth part of the latter's practical experience. Unfortunately, too, the few men of action—and they were very few indeed—were in the ranks of the Bolsheviks. With a few outstanding exceptions like Peter the Great, Russians had always found it easier to destroy than to create. Everything was against Kerensky. Even the French and British Governments, which had failed to understand the extent and nature of the revolution, were on the side of the generals and hampered Kerensky by demands which neither he nor, least of all, any general could fulfil. As M. Grenard, the French Consul-General in Moscow, who knew Russia well, wrote later: 'The Allies were blinded in their desire to prolong the military collaboration of Russia at all costs. They entirely failed to see what was possible at the moment and what was not. Thus they were simply playing into Lenin's hands and estranging Kerensky from the people.'

Regarding Petrograd as the centre of defeatism and looking for further support outside the capital, Kerensky convoked an unwieldy State Conference which was held in Moscow from August 25 to August 28.

In one respect Kerensky was right in coming to Moscow. The atmosphere there was not good, but it was infinitely better than the miasma in Petrograd. There had been virtually no disorders throughout the summer and, if there was little enthusiasm for the war, there was still less for Bolshevism. On the other hand, the size of the Conference condemned it to futility from the start. The delegates numbered over 2,000, including deputies of the four former Dumas and representatives of all parties and classes except the Bolsheviks and the Left-wing Mensheviks, who abstained.

An attempt by the Moscow Bolsheviks to organise a strike on the opening day failed dismally, and Kerensky's speech promising the sternest suppression of any attempted rising against the Government was well enough received. There was, however, an endless spate of oratory which was too much even for the Russians, and the only impression left on the minds of the people was the blunt language of General Kornilov demanding the strongest measures, including the suppression of soldiers' soviets and meetings, for the restoration of military discipline and the prevention of the complete collapse of the troops at the front.

The speech pleased the anti-Soviet *bourgeoisie* and, of course, the vast bulk of the army and naval officers. It alarmed the Socialist-Revolutionaries and Mensheviks throughout the country. To Lenin, who, after his two failures to seize power, had been waiting patiently and grimly for another opportunity, the speech must have brought a fierce gladness. The clash between Kerensky and Kornilov was to give him what he wanted.

It came with startling rapidity. Six days after the end of the Moscow State Conference the Germans took Riga and, by so doing, threatened Petrograd. This new menace alarmed the inhabitants of the capital and acted as a spur to the ambitions of General Kornilov who at once asked for the military garrison of Petrograd to be put under his control.

What happened from now on was a grim tragedy affecting the lives of millions and played out to the last with the appearance and appurtenances of *opéra bouffe*. Kerensky may not have been the strong man for whom all Russia, apart from the extreme Right and extreme Left, hoped, but, when it came to decision, he was at least the equal of General Kornilov, who, however gallant a commander in the field, was totally ignorant of politics and in the hour a crisis created by himself showed none of the attributes of a man of action, let alone a dictator.

Kerensky, who already had something more than a mere suspicion that even before the State Conference there had been talks at Army Headquarters of the necessity of a military dictatorship, was at that time uncertain whether Kornilov was party to a conspiracy or was being used by ambitious politicians and ex-ministers of the Provisional Government. He was unwilling to let Kornilov have control of the Petrograd garrison, but was agreeable to his being in charge of the Petrograd Military District.

He therefore sent Savinkov, who had now become Deputy Minister of War, to Army Headquarters to discuss with Kornilov the problems of handing over the army of the Petrograd Military District to the Commander-in-Chief, and also to arrange for the sending of a military force from the front to be at the disposal of the Provisional Government in connection with the proclamation of martial law, which had been rendered necessary by the capture of Riga by the Germans. Apart from the menace to the capital itself, there was an immense mass of refugees and deserters, and, in the event of a German advance, preliminary arrangements had been made for the transfer of the Government and the ministries to Moscow. Kerensky also gave to Savinkov implicit orders to request that the force which was to be sent to Petrograd should not include either the Caucasian 'Savage Division' or General Alexander Krymov, both being devoted to General Kornilov and therefore unreliable from the Government's point of view.

According to Savinkov, General Kornilov assured him on September 6 that he would carry out exactly the instructions of the Provisional Government. As Savinkov had also reported that on the previous day Kornilov had spoken harshly about the Government, it is doubtful whether his testimony is wholly reliable. He was a patriot and a man of action, but intrigue was in his blood, and in this tragically mismanaged affair there is little doubt that he saw his role as mediator between Kornilov and Kerensky and was, in fact, trying to unite them in spite of themselves.

Be this as it may, General Kornilov despatched the Cavalry Corps to Petrograd on September 7. At its head was the 'Savage Division'. General Krymov was in command of the whole force.

While Krymov's troops were approaching Petrograd, Prince V. N. Lvov,* who had been High Procurator of the Holy Synod in the first Provisional Government, arrived in Petrograd from Headquarters and requested an audience of Kerensky. Prince Lvov presented what he described as the orders of General Kornilov. They were that the Provisional Government should resign that evening and transfer its power to the general who would form a new Government. Kerensky and Savinkov were to leave at once for Headquarters. If they agreed, the general would give them ministerial posts in his Government. Otherwise he would not be responsible for their lives if they stayed in Petrograd. Kerensky refused, called the cabinet, which agreed to invest him with plenary powers, and ordered Kornilov by telegraph to surrender his post (September 9).

Kornilov replied with a pronouncement alleging that he was the victim of a frame-up by Kerensky, which was jeopardising the fate of Russia. 'I, General Kornilov, declare that

* Not the Prince who was the first premier of the Provisional Government.

under the pressure of the Bolshevik majority of the Soviets, the Provisional Government is acting in complete harmony with the plans of the German general staff and . . . undermining the very foundation of the country.'

If this was an exaggeration, so too was Kerensky's view of Kornilov's intentions. The most likely interpretation of this involved affair is that it was largely a misunderstanding, due to the two men's impetuosity and suspicions of one another, inflamed by the misleading information conveyed by the two intermediaries, V. N. Lvov and Savinkov. It seems that Kornilov actually wanted to move, not against the Government but against the Soviet, and especially against the Bolsheviks; in this action he thought he had obtained Kerensky's goodwill. Consequently his sudden dismissal seemed to him an act of betrayal, and he felt justified in refusing to obey it.

The affair ended in a disastrous fiasco. There was no fighting. The people of Petrograd, called to action by the Soviet, rose to defend themselves against what they were told was a 'counter-revolutionary plot'. General Krymov's 'Savage Division' melted away as it approached Petrograd, and its commander committed suicide. General Kornilov and a few other military leaders were arrested.

The Kornilov affair was the main turning-point in Russian history between the March and November Revolutions. It destroyed the last hope of anything approaching a free democratic system on Western lines.

General Kornilov had none of the constructive genius of a Bonaparte, and the people were against him from the start. His failure increased the prestige and swelled the ranks of the Bolsheviks, whose agitators had played a considerable part in his overthrow by persuading the troops of General Krymov to disobey the orders of their officers. Worst of all was the effect of the coup on the morale of the armed forces of the country. Regarded by the soldiers as a counter-revolutionary plot, the attempt created an irreparable gulf between the lower ranks and their officers. From now on no senior officer was trusted by the men, and in many parts of the country officers of all grades were murdered in the most brutal manner, the worst fate and the greatest savagery being reserved for the officers of the Russian Navy. The March Revolution which had overthrown Tsarism had been almost bloodless. From now on murder, rape and loot were to have free course.

Moreover, the attempted coup undermined fatally the already weak position of Kerensky who, by negotiating with Kornilov through Savinkov, had incurred the suspicion of the Left and, by abandoning the General, had lost the support of the Right. The political situation changed almost overnight. On September 12, the day of the collapse of the coup, Kerensky became Commander-in-Chief in addition to the other posts of Premier and Minister of War. On September 13 the Petrograd Soviet had for the first time a Bolshevik majority. On September 19 Moscow followed suit.

Kerensky was now more than ever at the mercy of the Soviet. Moreover, on account of the almost complete rupture between officers and men he was now completely bereft of any reliable military support. With the collapse of the army, Red Guards in civilian dress, with red brassards on their arms and carrying rifles, took the place of the soldiery.

To Lenin, who had, on Trotsky's admission, lost ground after the 'July Days', the Kornilov episode was a supernatural gift all the more precious because it was a complete surprise to him. In his glee he wrote from Finland to the Bolshevik Central Committee in Petrograd describing the affair as 'a most unexpected, really incredibly drastic turn of events'. Today, when Lenin is written up as an infallible demi-god by men who never knew him and who never saw the revolution, it is deviationism even to suggest that he did not plan every move months and even years ahead with the inspiration of genius. He made, of course, numerous mistakes and did not always show courage. He excelled, however, in taking advantage of the mistakes of his opponents, and these included all who disagreed with him on any point of his own interpretation and special brand of Marxism. And of all mistakes the Kornilov affair was the most valuable to Lenin and the most costly to his opponents.

To quote again Fernand Grenard, whom I knew intimately: 'At the critical hour the upper classes of Russia continued with their vague and illogical policy. They might have rallied all their forces, which were still great at that time, to the assistance of the temporary defenders of the state. They might have helped the Provisional Government to combat the terrible danger and the threat of disaster, plunder and massacre. They refrained from doing so, the majority of the ruling classes putting their hopes in a double blow: to have Kerensky killed by the Bolsheviks—who were supposed to be too weak to stand on their own—in order to beat the victors themselves on the day after their victory.'

This was only too true. I left Russia at the time of the Kornilov revolt, and already then many of my acquaintances in Moscow were saying that the only hope was to let the Bolsheviks in. They would not last a month, and their inevitable collapse would bring the people to their senses. When I returned at the end of the year as head of a special mission to the Bolshevik Government, some of my not very Right acquaintances were still propounding the same theory. By then the Bolsheviks had been *two* months in power.

Nearly two months were to elapse from the Kornilov failure to the collapse of the Kerensky Government. During this period the Government tried hard to build up its support, but had very little success. Educated people were in general apathetic, if not actually hostile. Meanwhile the Bolsheviks were growing stronger every day. It is undeniable that Kornilov's failure in September opened the door wide to the successful Revolution on November 7.

4

The November Revolution

LENIN, who was in Finland at the time of the Kornilov revolt, at first had some difficulty in convincing his colleagues on the Bolshevik Party's Central Committee that the new situation had, in his words, 'put armed insurrection on the agenda'. From his hiding-place he urged them not to delay. 'History will not forgive us if we do not take power now', he wrote. The slogan of 'All Power to the Soviets!', which he had temporarily shelved after the July Days, when the tide had gone against his party, was now revived and given a new meaning: power to the Soviets under Bolshevik control.

Lenin was insistent that the insurrection should be carried out before the Constituent Assembly met. At the elections, due to be held on November 12, the peasants would vote for the Socialist-Revolutionaries and overwhelm the proletarian Bolshevik vote. Moreover, the air was full of rumours of peace. Austria and even Germany were putting out feelers. Bulgaria had nearly had her fill of war. It was essential to the success of Bolshevism that he, Lenin, and no one else, least of all Kerensky, should give peace to the people.

Meanwhile Kerensky was endeavouring to form a new coalition ministry, but found himself hamstrung by deep differences over its composition. Some Socialists were reluctant to take part in a government with members of the Cadet Party, whom they suspected of sympathy for Kornilov. To decide the question a Democratic Conference was summoned for September 27. It was an unwieldy assembly, attended by some 1,600 delegates of various public organisations (soviets, trade unions, co-operatives, local councils, soldiers' representatives etc.). Most of those who attended were moderate Socialists, either Socialist-Revolutionaries or Mensheviks. On October 1, when the question of a new coalition was put to the vote, a majority of delegates first endorsed the idea in principle, and agreed to the participation of propertied elements, but then passed an amendment excluding the Cadets, the largest middle-class party. Finally, the entire motion was defeated. This made no sense whatever, and the conference broke up having achieved less than nothing.

The Government continued its talks with party leaders and a new coalition was eventually formed on October 8, but most of the ministers were little-known figures. Simultaneously a Council of the Republic came into being, consisting partly of former members of the Democratic Conference and partly of propertied persons nominated by the Government. Its purpose was to give the new Government at least the appearance of support until the elections for the Constituent Assembly were held. But the Council was obviously an artificial body without any real standing in the country, and soon proved itself unfit for its task. The constant talk only diverted attention from the need for decisive measures to deal with the mounting popular discontent and revolutionary turmoil.

At the opening session of the Council on October 7, Trotsky for the Bolsheviks delivered an uncompromising speech, accusing the *bourgeois* ministers of national treason, and led his supporters from the chamber. He was now chairman of the Petrograd Soviet, and also head of its Military Revolutionary Committee, which took charge of the detailed planning of the insurrection. The overall direction, of course, rested with Lenin, but he could not do much while he was out of Petrograd. On October 20, he arrived in the capital and went into hiding on the Vyborg side of the city. Three days later, on October 23, Lenin attended a secret meeting of the Bolshevik Central Committee at Sukhanov's flat and urged an immediate armed rising. The discussion was long, and he had to use all his powers of persuasion to convince his colleagues. But in the end his will prevailed. In the early hours of the morning Lenin, Trotsky, Dzerzhinsky, Uritsky, Sverdlov, Stalin, Bubnov, Sokolnikov, Lomov and Madame Kollontay voted in favour of the rising. Zinoviev, Lenin's companion in exile during the first years of the war, and Kamenev voted against. Of the ten Bolsheviks who voted for the October Revolution, all are now dead. Several of them were liquidated by Stalin.

Lenin and Trotsky were in character as far apart as the two poles. Lenin was a convinced Marxist who had adapted Marxism to Russian conditions. He was not interested in Western concepts of political liberty and of nationalism. He wanted a social revolution and, if he believed in the Marxist theory of the withering state, he regarded the proletarian revolution as the necessary prelude to Socialism. Having made up his mind, he was inflexible. In conversation with foreigners like myself he never lost his temper, nor was he personally vindictive like Stalin. If he promised anything, he fulfilled it, but, regarding capitalists as criminals, he considered it legitimate to deceive them.

Trotsky, dark with vast forehead, flashing eyes, sensuous mouth with well-trimmed beard and moustache, and beautiful well-manicured hands, looked unmistakably Jewish. Like Lenin he was short in stature with broad shoulders. Temperamentally he was an individualist with all the enthusiasms and depressions of an artist. When the sun smiled on him, he could be affable and even charming. When things went wrong, the clouds darkened his forehead, and his eyes flashed. He was a fierce hater, and in the later years of his life his venom was concentrated on Stalin. When Mr Wheeler-Bennett, the historian, went to see him in Mexico, he put a question about Stalin's part in the civil war. Trotsky thundered back: 'Stalin! Where was Stalin at the battle of Kazan?'

Again, like Lenin, Trotsky had lived abroad, knew several languages, and had an international culture which made him widely different from the Kremlin leaders of today. In political philosophy he was no match for Lenin. Nevertheless, it was typical of him that between the revolutions of 1905 and 1917 he had opposed Lenin on many occasions and had taken a line of his own, notably in regard to his theory of permanent revolution.

What brought the two men together was their passion for revolution. It was not until the so-called 'July Days' that Trotsky joined the Bolshevik Party. Then, as the chances of supreme power grew rosier, his enthusiasm for the cause became a consuming fire. To Lenin he brought the two indispensable qualities of great administrative ability and superb physical courage. During the 'July Days', he had saved Chernov, an opponent, from the wrath of the Kronstadt sailors, and when in 1918 the sailors came to the Ministry of War whilst I was with him and raised a clamour in the court outside, he excused himself to me and went out. A minute later I saw and heard him lashing the truculent and dangerous sailors with his tongue until they slunk away in shame. He was entirely alone.

Between October 23 and November 6 the Bolshevik propaganda against Kerensky was intensified daily. It was accompanied with the promise that, as soon as the Kerensky Government was overthrown, the peasants would be given the land, the workers would control the production and distribution of goods, and that peace would be made at once. Democratic liberties would be restored in full. 'The dictatorship of the proletariat and peasantry means the dictatorship of the toiling majority over the exploiting minority', wrote the leading Bolshevik daily on October 26. 'It would not use violence against the masses.'

At the same time the necessary preparations for the *coup d'état* were completed. On November 3 the Military Revolutionary Committee informed the Petrograd garrison that from now on it must obey only orders issued by the Committee. On the night of November 6, Lenin, putting on the wig which he used as a disguise, left his hiding-place and went to Smolny, in Tsarist days a seminary for young girls of good family, but now the headquarters of the Bolsheviks. Situated on the outskirts of the city it was guarded by Red Guards and armed sailors.

By this time Kerensky was aware that the insurrection was at hand and, announcing his intention to suppress it decisively, he tried to concentrate troops both in Petrograd and Moscow. He also appealed to the Council of the Republic, which although opposed to the insurrection showed itself pathetically helpless at the critical hour. It adopted a milk-and-water resolution proposed by the Menshevik leader Theodore Dan, which put the blame on the Government as well as the Bolsheviks and called for a committee of public safety to be set up, comprising members of the municipal council and the Left-wing parties. A Cadet resolution promising full support to the Government and insisting on firm measures to suppress the revolt was not put to the vote. Kerensky regarded the Council's attitude as a demonstration of non-confidence, which indeed it was.

During the night of November 6–7, armed detachments of Red Guards and pro-Bolshevik soldiers and sailors, obeying the orders of the Military Revolutionary Committee, occupied all the important points in the city, including the railway-stations, post office and telephone exchange, food stores, banks and the strategic bridges across the Neva. When the military district headquarters ordered the bridges to be raised, 200 Red Guards ensured that they were promptly lowered again. The cruiser *Aurora*, manned by revolutionary sailors from Kronstadt, sailed up the river and disembarked reinforcements at the Nikolayevsky Quay. There was no resistance or blood-shed, since nearly all the troops in the Petrograd garrison were sympathetic to the insurgents. A few units remained neutral, notably three regiments of Cossacks from the Don. When they received a telegram ordering them to assist the Government and 'the Soviets of revolutionary democracy', they played for time, asking whether the infantry would advance with them, and then announced that they would not fight alone 'as they did not want to act as human targets'.

In the Winter Palace, the vast former residence of the Tsars on the south bank of the Neva, the Government remained in continuous session, issuing orders and appeals to which no one paid much attention. On the morning of November 7, Kerensky left the building in an open car, escorted by a second vehicle flying the American flag, in quest of reinforcements. No attempt was made to stop him. The insurgents hesitated to attack the Palace, one of the few important buildings they had failed to seize during the night. It was defended by some Cossacks, military cadets and a battalion of brave but ineffectual women soldiers. By nightfall it had been surrounded and communications with the outside world all but interrupted. An ultimatum was issued in the name of the Petrograd Soviet giving the Government twenty minutes to surrender, threatening that otherwise the Palace would be bombarded.

In addition to the *Aurora* and other ships in the Neva, the insurgents now commanded the fortress of Peter and Paul across the river, with its powerful but ancient gun batteries. At 11 o'clock several dozen shells were fired at the Palace, only a few of which struck the target. The defenders saw that their cause was hopeless and surrendered or dispersed as the insurgents gradually made their way into the enormous building. At 2 a.m. a group of men led by V. A. Antonov-Ovseyenko burst into the room where the cabinet was in session. The ministers were arrested and marched off to the fortress of Peter and Paul. They were not treated badly, for the Bolsheviks had no wish to cause unnecessary bloodshed at this early stage.

On November 8, a new Government was formed, the Council of People's Commissars, with Lenin as chairman, Trotsky as People's Commissar for Foreign Affairs and the still little-known Stalin as People's Commissar for Nationalities. For some days life in Petrograd continued more or less normally. Shops and cinemas stayed open, and on the surface there was little indication that Russia had passed a decisive turning-point in her history.

In Petrograd at least, the November Revolution was hardly the titanic struggle between the forces of light and darkness that it has sometimes been made out to be. The numbers of men engaged were small, and there was a good deal of inefficiency and improvisation on both sides. The Bolsheviks achieved power with almost ridiculous ease. Petrograd was, of course, not Russia. In Moscow there was fighting for a week before the insurgents captured the city, and drove from its ancient Kremlin the 5,000 officer cadets who had taken possession of it. There was a certain amount of violence in several other cities, and even after they had formally passed under the control of local workers' and soldiers' soviets the authority of the new régime rested very lightly.

The chief potential centre of resistance in the early days of the Revolution, naturally enough, was the army, strung out along the Western front. But discipline had been so undermined by November that few units were in a position to act decisively. Kerensky's efforts to relieve Petrograd with the aid of a few hundred Cossacks ended in utter failure on November 12. As at the time of the Kornilov affair two months earlier, the troops were prevented from advancing by the railwaymen, who thought that by obstructing them they could avoid the outbreak of civil war. The new Commander-in-Chief, General Dukhonin, called on all the democratic forces of the nation to unite and elect a government with real authority to speak for Russia. The Bolsheviks replied by ordering him to start talks with representatives of the German High Command. When he refused, an expedition was sent against him led by a junior officer, ensign Krylenko, who was nominated Supreme Commander of the Russian armed forces. On December 3, Dukhonin was killed by a sailor. Army Headquarters at Moghilev passed under Bolshevik control.

Those elements in the army most strongly opposed to the November Revolution, mainly officers, made their way with some difficulty to the territory of the Don Cossacks in southern Russia, where a new centre of resistance came into being. Among those who reached this area was General Kornilov, who had been released from captivity after the Revolution. Together with other generals he helped to organise a 'Volunteer Army' and approached the Western Allies for support. His forces came to be called 'Whites' in opposition to the 'Reds' who backed the Bolsheviks.

So began a bitter civil war which was to last for nearly three years and cost many hundreds of thousands of lives. Both sides committed terrible atrocities. Although the Whites received some aid in men, money and equipment from friendly Allied Powers, the fortunes of war went against them, and by 1921 the Bolsheviks—or Communists, as they now called themselves—were undisputed masters of most of the former Russian Empire. The Revolution exacted a heavy price from the Russian people, and indeed from the Communists themselves. It left a legacy of bitterness and hatred that makes itself felt to this day.

Before considering the long-term consequences of the November Revolution, we must inquire why the Bolsheviks were able to win and hold power in 1917. The simplest explanation is that they had a better idea than their adversaries of what they wanted and were more resolute in enforcing their will. It might be argued that they only succeeded by default—because their adversaries made so many mistakes. Once Tsarism had been overthrown, the democratic forces showed themselves sadly divided. The Provisional Government received only half-hearted backing from the moderate Socialists in the Soviet. Kerensky, who tried to steer a middle course between hostile pressures from the Left and from the Right, could have survived only on one condition: that the British and French Governments had allowed him to make an honourable separate peace.

Instead, the military representatives of the Western Powers helped to bring about his defeat by urging him to undertake offensives which brought little benefit to the West and merely increased the number of his opponents. Such a peace would have cost Russia less than that she was eventually forced to conclude. Admittedly it would have been difficult to convince public opinion of its necessity at the time, and Kerensky would no doubt have been denounced as a traitor in many quarters, particularly by Right-wing politicians. But these groups did not show themselves to be possessed of much foresight in the autumn of 1917. Many reactionaries and disillusioned Liberals clung to the view that the Bolsheviks, if they took power, would commit political suicide within a few weeks.

Moreover, the Bolsheviks entered the struggle with certain advantages which deserve to be noted more fully. In the first place they were skilled propagandists, adept at concealing their intentions behind an inoffensive mask which could deceive the unwary. It was characteristic that in October Trotsky took care to present each successive challenge to the Provisional Government's authority by the Military Revolutionary

Committee as a legitimate act of self-defence by 'revolutionary democracy' against 'the threat of counter-revolution'. This gave the insurgents a feeling of righteousness and embarrassed the defenders of the status quo. The sheer volume of the invective hurled by the Bolsheviks against the Provisional Government had its effect. Many people took the view that, even if some of their charges were exaggerated, 'there's no smoke without fire'. A number of those who did not sympathise with the Bolsheviks' aims were nevertheless willing to believe the aspersions they cast upon Kerensky and other democratic leaders.

The general atmosphere in Petrograd at this time was one of suspicion which sometimes verged on hysteria. Credence was generously given to wild rumours which in more normal times would have been discountenanced. The war, with all the suffering and violence it entailed, had aroused emotions to fever pitch, and extremists could successfully appeal to deep-rooted aspirations—and prejudices—among the broad mass of the population.

Lenin frequently emphasised the importance of simple slogans. Inscribed on hundreds of symbolic red banners, held aloft during protest marches through the streets, they helped to focus popular grievances and gained force by continual repetition. In this way large numbers of Russians who until recently had scarcely heard of the Bolshevik Party could be induced to accept its leadership and even to identify themselves with it. Most workers and peasant soldiers in 1917 were rather naive in political matters. They did not realise that some issues were too complex for radical solutions, and that if they insisted on such action they might create more problems than they solved.

The chief themes emphasised in Bolshevik propaganda between the March and November Revolutions were bread, land and peace. Undoubtedly the most effective slogan was 'Peace to the Huts, War to the Palaces!'. It left open the question of the kind of peace that they, the Bolsheviks, would accept if they came to power. Nearly all Russians, especially those in uniform, were eager for a speedy democratic peace, but very few of them wanted to conclude a separate peace with the powerful German Empire, which would involve Russia in the loss of considerable territory and, as it was thought, virtually turn her into a satellite of the Central Powers.

Lenin's argument was that once the Bolsheviks were victorious they would invite all belligerents to join in peace talks. If they refused, the onus for prolonging hostilities would fall upon their Governments, which would soon be brought to see reason by their own peoples. The Revolution in Russia would be followed very rapidly by proletarian uprisings in the advanced industrial countries of the West, especially Germany. Once the Kaiser had been overthrown, German and Russian Socialists would be free to work out an honourable, democratic peace settlement.

But what would happen if this calculation proved over-optimistic? What if the Allied Powers, regarding the Bolsheviks as usurpers and traitors to the common cause, were to ignore their proposals, while the revolution in Germany were to be delayed? In such a situation revolutionary Russia, bereft of her army, would find herself confronted with the whole might of German 'imperialism'. She would either have to accept extremely onerous peace terms or else let herself be occupied and fight a guerilla war.

This was precisely the situation that the Bolshevik Government faced in March, 1918, when it was obliged to accept the treaty of Brest-Litovsk, imposed upon it by the Germans—'a robbers' peace', as Lenin himself called it, which if its terms had been implemented fully would soon have ruined Russia and brought his régime tumbling. Had the soldiers in 1917 known what was implied in the simple slogan of 'peace', one may doubt whether they would have responded to it quite so enthusiastically. Moreover, the civil war which the Bolsheviks offered in lieu of the international war was to involve more fighting than most of them bargained for.

The same disappointments awaited those who thought that Bolshevik rule would give the land to the peasants and the factories to the workers. It is true that decrees to this effect were issued shortly after the new régime took over. The landowners and industrialists were expropriated. But the peasants soon found themselves deprived of the right to trade in their produce, which was confiscated by squads of armed men from the cities who could offer them little or nothing of value in exchange. The workers soon found their control of industry reduced to a fiction, for it led to anarchy and a near-total stoppage of production. This the Bolsheviks could not tolerate, and they therefore began to build up a centralised administrative machine for planning and management. These officials gave orders which the workers in the factories had to obey.

Similarly, the non-Russian minorities, who took at its face value the Bolshevik slogan of national self-determination and hoped that they would be able to form independent states after the Revolution, soon found that in practice their rights were very narrowly circumscribed. They were told that the interests of the proletarian revolution had to come first, and what these interests were only Moscow could decide. In the event only those nations that could rely on effective support from foreign Powers, such as the Poles, Finns and the Baltic peoples, were able to preserve their independence in the civil war of 1918–20 and to resist the Bolsheviks' efforts to bring them into their 'federation of Soviet republics'. To those nations that were absorbed the Soviet constitution afforded far-reaching autonomy, but this existed largely on paper. For the Communists who ruled over these areas took their orders from the leaders of the All-Union Communist Party in Moscow, which looked askance at any manifestation of 'bourgeois nationalism'.

Before the November Revolution the Bolsheviks took care to present themselves as good democrats, who were doing little more than to reflect the natural revolutionary impulses of the masses. Their slogan was 'All Power to the Soviets!'. At this time the Soviets were indeed genuinely popular organs, whose executive members maintained close ties with the workers in the factories who elected them.

But the Bolsheviks did not consider themselves in any way bound by the people's will where this seemed likely to obstruct their own plans for building Socialism. They looked on the

Soviets as useful instruments for gaining power, but once they had performed this task they sought to bring them under firm Party control. Pressure was brought to bear for the re-election of Soviets which did not toe the line. At these elections the balloting was strictly supervised, so that only those candidates considered politically reliable had a chance. This process of 'bolshevisation' took several months. It was reflected in the composition and rights of the national Congress of Soviets and its Central Executive Committee.

By the summer of 1918 these bodies consisted entirely of Bolsheviks, and their governmental powers were progressively whittled away. Already within a few months of the Revolution the most important decisions were taken by a handful of men at the summit of the Party hierarchy, and then transmitted down to the masses through a complex network of administrative organs. Formally, the governmental structure was democratic, but in practice it was dictatorial. The constitutional provisions served to obscure the fact that the real centre of power was at the top. It is difficult to say how far this development was deliberate, and how far the Bolsheviks themselves were victims of their own propaganda—that is to say, having convinced themselves that they had achieved a near-perfect system of 'Socialist democracy', they were blind to its faults and incapable of taking measures to improve it.

The second major reason for the Bolsheviks' success was their superior Party discipline. Among other things this enabled their leaders to adopt a more flexible tactical course, since there was less risk of their being criticised for inconsistency. This tactical flexibility was combined with a single-minded concentration upon the main strategic aim, the conquest and consolidation of their power.

As we have seen, Lenin responded very rapidly to sudden changes in the political climate, for instance to the opportunities opened up by Kornilov's revolt. Although his Party comrades did not always agree with him, his position of personal pre-eminence among them ensured that in 1917 disagreements were short-lived and open splits usually avoided; if they did nevertheless occur, the errant members soon came to confess their errors and were received back into the fold without much fuss. At a lower level the rank-and-file Party members were by and large content to carry out the orders they received from the centre, which still left them plenty of scope for personal initiative. The Bolshevik Party in 1917 was not the soulless apparatus it was to become later under Stalin.

This discipline compensated for their relative weakness in numbers. At the time of the November Revolution the Bolsheviks had no more than about 250,000 firmly-committed adherents—this in a country with a population of some 165 million! The Socialist-Revolutionaries were incomparably stronger, but their lack of discipline was a by-word. They were split into three major factions and several sub-groups. The Mensheviks, too, were divided between a Left-wing and a Right-wing faction. Lenin saw it as his task to exploit these divisions, winning the active support of some groups, neutralising others, and isolating those most opposed to him, until his Party was strong enough to absorb or crush each one in turn. It was an operation that called for a high degree of political skill and an acute sense of timing.

The crucial phase came immediately after the November Revolution, when the Bolsheviks were dangerously isolated and the moderate Socialists still enjoyed a good deal of political freedom. The latter were sincerely opposed to minority dictatorship, but could not make their opposition politically effective. At the second All-Russian Congress of Soviets, which met in the evening of November 7, moderate Socialists held about one-third of the seats. Of 650 deputies only 390 were Bolsheviks, and many of them thought Lenin's policy of seizing power unduly risky.

The democratic groups, if they had played their cards well, could have made things awkward for the Bolsheviks by showing clearly that they were usurpers. But at the first session the Mensheviks and Right-wing Socialist-Revolutionaries were content to protest by withdrawing from the chamber, to the accompaniment of a hail of choice abuse from Trotsky. This feeble gesture left the field clear for their opponents. At the next session on November 8, the Congress passed Lenin's famous land and peace decrees with scarcely a dissentient voice, confirmed in office the new all-Bolshevik Government, and promptly adjourned. Lenin could now claim with some plausibility that his régime, which owed its existence to an act of force, had the approval of the people's representatives. He could also take the credit for moves towards peace and agrarian reform—although the land decree was, as he admitted, hastily copied from a document compiled under the influence of his old rivals, the Socialist-Revolutionaries.

Despite this setback the moderate Socialists entered into negotiations for a coalition government—a plan favoured by some Bolshevik leaders, notably Kamenev and Zinoviev. None of those who participated in these talks realised that Lenin had no intention of allowing them to succeed. He allowed them to talk only in order to buy time, and prevent the moderate Socialists coming to the aid of the anti-Bolshevik forces. A few days later, when the Bolsheviks had won control of Moscow and other major provincial centres, he felt strong enough to declare his hand.

Shortly afterwards, however, he changed his line once again. The elections to the Constituent Assembly had now been duly held, and he knew that only a small minority of the deputies would be Bolsheviks. He therefore deemed it expedient to come to an arrangement with the Left-wing Socialist-Revolutionaries, who had formally split off from their parent body. Five members of this party were admitted to the Government. They were unable to exercise much moderating influence upon Bolshevik policy, but their presence was valuable to Lenin since it made his régime look more broadly based than it was. When the Left Socialist-Revolutionary ministers resigned in March, 1918, in protest against the treaty of Brest-Litovsk, he had no regrets, since by then they had outlived their usefulness.

As for the Constituent Assembly, Lenin reluctantly allowed it to meet for a single session on January 18–19, 1918. The Bolsheviks had only 168 out of 703 deputies; the Socialist-Revolutionaries had 380 representatives, the Left Socialist-Revolutionaries thirty-nine, the national minority parties eighty-one and the Mensheviks eighteen. Armed soldiers and sailors were introduced into the gallery of the debating-chamber, and the proceedings were held under the continual threat of violence.

The Left Socialist-Revolutionaries backed a Bolshevik motion calling on the Assembly to endorse unconditionally the policies of the Soviet Government. When this was rejected the deputies of these two parties withdrew. The other deputies went on talking until 5 a.m., when a sailor from Kronstadt, Zhelezniakov, head of the militia company nominally in charge of the members' security, requested the chairman, Chernov, to suspend the session 'because the guards are tired'. Later that morning the Assembly was formally dissolved. In defence of his actions Lenin argued that the elections had been unfair and that the Soviets represented a higher form of democracy than the allegedly *bourgeois* Assembly. But the real fault of the Assembly in Bolshevik eyes was that, had it endured, it might have afforded a platform for political opposition, and exposed the hollowness of their claim to embody the true interests of the working masses.

The third point in the Bolsheviks' favour in 1917 was that they possessed a coherent ideology. They saw themselves as bringing to fulfilment the original vision of Karl Marx, that the workers would one day rise in revolt against their capitalist exploiters and build a new Socialist society, in which justice and harmony would prevail—a kind of earthly kingdom of God, or utopia. This messianic, prophetic element in Marxism had always been particularly attractive to Russian intellectuals, with their liking for extreme solutions and their optimistic belief in the ultimate perfectibility of man. Lenin, while taking from Marx only what he needed to justify his own actions and disregarding whatever did not suit him, at the same time rather inconsistently regarded Marx as a universal genius who had provided a final, truly scientific answer to the problems of revolutionary social change. He had supposedly discovered the laws governing the working of human society, and made it possible for a gifted leader who applied his method to understand them and, by shaping his conduct accordingly, to achieve success.

In practical terms this ideological way of thinking gave the Bolsheviks a mood of self-confident activism, a dynamic élan, which was denied to their rivals. They felt that history was on their side and final victory assured. Even if they themselves might die in the attempt, their self-sacrifice would be justified by the glorious achievements of the Socialist future. One might almost say that they acted like men possessed, or like the votaries of some strange religious sect, convinced that they alone held the key to the True Gospel. They were ready to submerge their own individual egos in the collective will of the Party, to make superhuman efforts for the good of their cause.

The Bolsheviks saw themselves as a chosen élite, freed from the ethical restraints that applied to other men in accomplishing their will. The supreme end of the Revolution justified any means that served it. They were ready to use violence and trickery on an unparalleled scale where they thought that by doing so they would promote their objectives. In their eyes the sole test of the merits of any action was its expediency. If it worked, then it was 'correct'; and the decision as to whether it worked or not was made, not by themselves from observation of the facts, but by higher authority. For they reasoned that the judgment of any individual was likely to be faulty; wisdom rested with the collective—in effect, with the Party leadership. They themselves were of little account; their *raison d'être* was to serve a higher purpose.

This picture of the Bolshevik mind of course to some extent represents an ideal rather than the reality. Not all followers of Lenin thought or behaved in this almost inhuman way in 1917. There were among them kindly individuals who shrank from ruthless measures, and careerists who put their own interest before that of the Party. But it is to this ideological commitment that one must look for the real secret of their success. The Bolsheviks won because they were the first to develop the political techniques that we commonly describe today as 'totalitarian', meaning the manipulation of human beings and ideas on a massive and all-pervading scale. These techniques were later to be refined by Stalin and to be applied by other parties and governments outside Russia, both Communist and non-Communist.

Against a totalitarian movement it is difficult for men who respect liberal and democratic values to prevail—difficult, but by no means impossible, as the course of twentieth-century history has shown. It was Russia's tragedy that in 1917, in the midst of a World War and burdened by the heavy legacy of Tsarism, she was pathetically ill-equipped to advance along the road to freedom and responsible government. Instead she took the path of dictatorship—with results that were to come as a surprise to most Russians who lived through the Revolutions of 1917.

The Achievements of
the Russian Revolution

by John Keep

REVOLUTIONS, like wars, seldom have the results so confidently anticipated by those who launch them. The truth of
this maxim has been amply demonstrated by the history of
Russia and of international Communism over the past fifty
years. The most significant achievement of the November Revolution has been to build a powerful modern State in place of
the ramshackle empire of the Tsars. Today the Soviet leaders
have at their disposal vast resources of political, military and
economic strength. The USSR is the chief rival of the United
States in a struggle for global supremacy. It has an advanced
ramified industry, based upon a high level of scientific and
technological expertise, and an impressive defence potential.
Its government seems firmly entrenched and controls every
aspect of the nation's intellectual life.

Yet national grandeur, political stability and economic
development were not among the slogans which the Bolsheviks
inscribed upon their banners in 1917. Their principal objective
was to bring about worldwide proletarian revolution, which
would usher in the international classless society. For Lenin
the Bolshevik seizure of power in Russia was simply a means
to a greater end. He believed that it would be followed, within
a matter of months, by the advent of the working class to power
in more advanced countries, which had a higher level of
economic and cultural development, and according to Marxist
criteria were better prepared for Socialism. He did not then
think that Soviet Russia could survive as an isolated 'workers'
State' in a hostile capitalist environment; still less that she
could go on to build Socialism within her borders without aid

from abroad, largely under the direction of the Communist Party, from above rather than from below; and that she would try to bring about the international revolution mainly by utilising the vast power of her State. Yet this was what actually came to pass.

Soviet historians have claimed that Lenin's theory provided for such eventualities, and that they are compatible with the 'objective laws of history' as defined by Marx and Engels. Nothing could be farther from the truth. In 1917 the Bolsheviks took a gamble, which came off—but in a way they did not bargain for. History denied them international revolution, but put at their disposal great reserves of untapped energy within Russia itself. This enabled them to crush their adversaries and to go far in re-shaping Russian society according to their own design. They showed themselves most skilful in improvising policies to meet the situation they faced, and then justifying their actions in terms of Marxist or Leninist theory.

This doctrinal flexibility enabled them to survive, to consolidate their power, and then to extend it on a scale unimaginable in 1917. But it was bought at a high price. It meant that they had to abandon many of their cherished ideals and adjust themselves to the harsh logic of power. They had to convert themselves from a party of revolutionaries to a party of government. They had to rule over a population that was largely apathetic or hostile, and which they could not wholly trust. They had to use dictatorial methods, more ruthless than those of the Tsars, and to borrow some of their predecessors' techniques for keeping the people in order.

The history of Soviet Russia makes sense only when one bears in mind this gulf between practice and precept, between action and theory. The Bolsheviks could not afford openly to admit that they were departing from their original principles, as this would have led people to question the basis for their rule, their legitimacy. Instead they maintained the contrary and compelled everyone to believe that theirs was the only conceivable form of government for Russia, and that it enjoyed universal support—even though this meant launching a massive drive to indoctrinate the people with these ideas, and virtually isolating them from all external independent sources of information. Regardless of cost, they endeavoured to bolster the official ideology, and to draw a veil of deliberate obfuscation at all those points where it was in conflict with reality. Truth had to give way to fiction.

Eventually Russia became a land of make-believe, in which people were required to deny the evidence of their senses and to think as they were ordered—or else run the risk of serious trouble. They had to learn to suppress any heretical notions and to shape their conduct, outwardly at least, in accordance with the will of the ruling Communist Party or its leader. They had to develop a public personality which conformed to the official image of the way that a loyal Soviet citizen ought to behave. In the world outside an ugly new term came into use to describe this ugly state of affairs: totalitarianism.

In the USSR totalitarian pressures were most intense in the 1930s and again after the end of the Second World War. After Stalin's death in 1953 his successors slightly relaxed their demands upon the ordinary citizen, and began to court his favour in the hope of overcoming the potentially dangerous gulf between the rulers and the ruled. But it soon became clear that this 'liberalisation' had to be confined within very narrow limits, unless the myths whereby the régime sustained itself were to be undermined and the whole edifice imperilled. The policy adopted was an unsatisfactory compromise. Today, fifty years after the November Revolution, the leaders of the Communist Party and the Soviet State are grappling with an insoluble problem: how to reconcile their continuing dictatorship with their subjects' natural aspirations for basic human values, rights and freedoms—in fact, for the very ideals in the name of which the Bolsheviks once seized power.

It will thus be apparent that, in considering the achievements of the Revolution, we are confronted with something of a paradox. Many of the gains that have been registered are not wholly or directly attributable to actions taken by the Communist régime, but official spokesmen are quick to appropriate the credit for every advance. For example, there is no doubt that the Soviet Government has fostered a very rapid rate of economic growth; but *some* economic progress would have taken place in Russia over the past half-century *whatever* her form of government.

Unless we take account of possible alternatives, we cannot arrive at a fair assessment of the Communists' actual share in this development. Conversely, some of the most important results of the Revolution have been incidental to the Bolsheviks' aims or even in sharp contrast to them. These, too, need to be taken into consideration. It would of course be unfair to put the blame for every reverse or disappointment on the Soviet régime, which like any other is partly subject to circumstances outside its control. But in view of the extravagant claims advanced by the Soviet Communists on their own behalf, it is worth pointing out that men have to bear the responsibility for all the consequences of their actions, both good and bad, before the bar of history.

Let us examine first the international setting in which the Soviet Union has attempted to pursue its revolutionary objectives over the past fifty years.

Already in 1918, by signing with Imperial Germany the treaty of Brest-Litovsk, which took Russia out of the First World War, Lenin showed a realistic awareness that the interests of international Communism had to be subordinated to the interests of preserving Soviet Russia, as the homeland and 'advance base' of world revolution. When the Third International (Comintern) was set up in the following year, he left no stone unturned to ensure that it should be under the firm control of the Soviet Communist Party, its largest and most important component.

From 1921 onwards, faced with a well-entrenched *bourgeois* political and social order in the rest of Europe, the Soviet Government placed more overt emphasis upon conventional diplomacy and less upon subversive activities. It strove hard to give its relations with capitalist states a semblance of normality, and especially to develop economic links with them, despite the obvious differences in their social and political systems. In the mid-1930s Soviet Russia dropped her earlier hostility to the League of Nations and entered into alliances with some non-Communist states against others that threatened her security, chiefly Nazi Germany. This policy led logically to Soviet Russia's role as a leading member of the Grand Alliance which defeated Hitler in the Second World War.

But these shifts of tactics did not imply any modification of long-term strategic aims, as some people in the West rather naively thought at the time. They meant only that world revolution was now viewed by the Soviet leaders in a different perspective. Already Lenin had envisaged a fairly lengthy period of 'peaceful co-existence' with capitalist states. Stalin was even less sanguine about the chances of revolutions coming to pass in the near future as a result of efforts by local Communist forces. These were everywhere still very weak—partly because Stalin himself insisted on them preserving their doctrinal purity at all costs, even if this meant losing popular support. Instead he attached much importance to the aid which the Soviet State, with its powerful armed forces, could give native Communists when war brought the opportunity for intervention in their countries' affairs.

Stalin actually distrusted strongly-based local Communist movements, because they would be more difficult for him to control. This calculation was borne out by the course of events from 1944 to 1949. In a number of East European countries the Red Army was able to bring local Communists to power, and to maintain them in office, by force or the threat of force, and to do so without entering into a major conflict with the Western Powers, which had been weakened by the war. On the other hand, in such countries as Yugoslavia—and more significantly, China—where the Communist revolution did not rest simply on Soviet bayonets, but could draw upon strong indigenous sources of support, Stalin could not make his will prevail unconditionally.

When Stalin died he bequeathed to his heirs what seemed to be the most formidable empire known to history. It stretched from the Elbe and the Danube to the jungles of Vietnam and embraced about one-third of the world's inhabitants. Yet very soon cracks began to appear in the monolith. Today, fourteen years later, the Communist *bloc* is rent by profound schisms, of which that between Moscow and Peking is the most important. This has been a perfectly logical occurrence. For the Soviet model of development was imposed upon its satellites arbitrarily and artificially, without regard for the differences in their national traditions and requirements; once the central lynch-pin of the system was removed, it was bound to fall apart. In the long term an international union of states is incompatible with adherence to a rigid ideology, such as Communism insists on. It can endure only so long as there is a single centre of power with unchallenged authority to interpret disputed points of doctrine, to lay down the tactical line for the movement as a whole. This centre no longer exists.

The only other way to run an empire is by giving it a constitutional framework, ensuring that the rights of each member-state are clearly defined in law and are respected by others. It is conceivable that the Communist Powers, or some of them, may evolve some such international legal system. But if they do, the nature of Communism will itself have changed. It would cease to be a quasi-religious movement, whose members feel that their higher vocation entitles them to enforce their will by unlimited violence. They would have to put aside as utopian the dream of re-making the world in their own image and allow the countries they rule to become more or less normal, peace-loving members of the international community.

It is still much too early to say whether such a development is likely to occur, since this depends largely on the response which other Powers make to the Communist challenge. After fifty years of struggle to extend their influence abroad, the Soviet leaders can derive a fair amount of satisfaction at their achievements. Although only one country, Cuba, has actually acquired a Communist government in recent years, the number of Party members and sympathisers is continually growing, particularly in the developing lands. At the 23rd congress of the Soviet Communist Party in March, 1966, there were said to be eighty-eight Communist parties in the world with some 50 million adherents. Such statistics help to fortify the official Soviet belief that history is bearing out their original expectations, even if in a devious way. The current analysis which they make of the world situation lays great emphasis upon the 'struggle for peace' in a nuclear age and the 'national-liberation movement' in the colonial or newly independent countries, in both of which Communists are allotted a spearhead role.

As Moscow sees it, the present balance of world strategic power allows the USSR to extend its political influence without great risk of war, since in the last resort the Western democracies will shrink from resolute military counter-measures, fearing annihilation and hostile popular reactions. As for the developing countries, their nationalist régimes are seen as approximately where Kerensky was in the autumn of 1917: the revolution has reached its *bourgeois* or 'national-democratic' stage and is now moving into the phase of Socialism—that is to say, coming under Communist control. When this occurs, it is thought that the position of Western 'imperialism' will become untenable. Deprived of the vast profits supposedly gained from colonial or neo-colonial exploitation, the Western *bourgeoisie* will be unable to satisfy the rising economic demands of the workers. This will enhance the appeals of Soviet-style Communism, which will be able to offer the Western masses not only material abundance, but also the prospect of lasting peace through disarmament, controlled by a Moscow-dominated world authority. In this way Lenin's vision of world revolution will be realised, perhaps without the social convulsions he expected.

How far does this analysis fit the facts? Clearly, it omits from consideration many aspects of the contemporary world scene, only a few of which can be mentioned here. Western pacifist or neutralist movements become discredited if they accept overt Communist leadership. The USSR's popular appeal in the advanced countries is limited by its rejection of democratic values. The major capitalist Powers still have vast untapped resources which they can draw upon to maintain economic progress and political stability. Most developing countries have rejected Communism in favour of some kind of Socialist nationalism which corresponds more closely to their own needs, so that despite much effort the USSR has not yet brought the anti-colonial revolution under its firm control. Finally, the Communist countries are experiencing much difficulty in maintaining their own cohesion and in competing effectively with the West.

Where this analysis is particularly deficient is in its neglect of the time factor. If a large number of impoverished countries adhered to the Communist *bloc*, this would impose a tremendously heavy burden upon its strained resources, which even at optimum rates of development would take generations of effort to satisfy. The peoples of Asia, Africa and Latin America could provide ample reserves of manpower and revolutionary zeal, but this is a poor substitute for the industrial strength and technical skill of the Western proletariat. Indeed, their very immaturity is likely to raise political problems, since they may prefer the ultra-revolutionary Chinese point of view on world affairs to that of the Soviets.

Historical experience suggests that it is the Communist countries, rather than the Western Powers, which have most to fear from the passage of time. For as they achieve a degree of maturity it becomes increasingly difficult for their leaders to maintain their revolutionary ideology undefiled, and to convince people at home and abroad that Marxism-Leninism provides the only correct solution to their current problems. The closer Communism approaches its final goal, the more outdated its ideas appear.

Let us now turn to the impact of Communism within Russia itself. The early Bolsheviks held that changes in the economic basis of society would bring in their train corresponding changes in its 'superstructure'—in political institutions and the ideas that men held. But in fact Soviet economic development has owed a great deal to direction from above, to decisions taken by the Party leadership. Contrary to Marxist teaching, in the USSR 'politics commands', not economics. Industrial growth was seen as necessary to ensure the security of the régime against internal and external enemies. The working class which Russia so singularly lacked before 1917, and on which the Communists professedly intended to base their power, had to be created by a deliberate act of policy.

By bringing industry, agriculture and trade under centralised State control, and by scientifically planning the production and distribution of goods, the Soviet leaders hoped to achieve a rate of growth far more rapid than that in capitalist countries, which were subject to the fluctuations of supply and demand inherent in a free-enterprise market economy. But their ideas on the regulation of economic life under Socialism were at first very vague. Marx had said little about such questions, on the grounds that the correct policies would be formulated by the workers themselves on the basis of their practical experience. Thus the Bolsheviks' efforts to institute and manage a planned economy were very experimental. They had to grope in the dark, and were in a sense less fortunate than other Socialist countries since, which have had the opportunity to learn from their mistakes.

These trial-and-error methods were much in evidence during the years of civil war (1918–20). Flushed with revolutionary enthusiasm, and believing that Communism was just around the corner, the Bolsheviks embarked upon a policy of expropriating the property of 'class enemies' wholesale and trying to control every kind of economic activity, even though the means of doing so were clearly lacking. This extremism was also partly due to expediency, to the overriding need to keep the Red Army and the régime in being at a time of general scarcity.

In 1921, faced with famine and popular revolt, Lenin introduced the so-called 'New Economic Policy' (NEP). Under this system the State kept control of the 'commanding heights' of the economy but tolerated a certain amount of private trade and small-scale industrial enterprise; the peasants were allowed to sell their surplus produce on the free market, after payment of taxes, and to choose the form of land tenure they wished. This period of uneasy co-existence between the private and public sectors of the economy lasted until 1928, by which time industrial and agricultural output had been restored to the pre-war level, and in some cases had exceeded it.

Stalin now decided that the time had come to launch a

full-scale assault upon the economy. The First Five-year Plan (1928–32) was a veritable second revolution, even more catastrophic in its impact than that of 1917. It was officially seen as a great leap forward along the road to industrialisation and Socialism. Emphasis was laid upon the construction of large-scale enterprises such as iron and steel works, which needed a lot of capital investment. To provide the requisite labour force millions of peasants were drafted into the factory compounds, where they lived and worked under grim conditions. By forcing people to superhuman feats of endurance, and by invoking the fanaticism of Party zealots, Stalin hoped to accomplish miracles within a very short time. He called upon the nation to develop 'a high Bolshevik tempo of construction' in order to overcome Russia's historic backwardness. 'We are fifty to a hundred years behind the advanced countries', he said in 1931. 'We must make good this distance in ten years, or else we shall be crushed.'

When the Nazis invaded in 1941 these seemed prescient words. One may readily agree that the First Five-year Plan and its successor (1933–7) created the industrial might without which the USSR would certainly have gone down to defeat at Hitler's hands. But there is no way of measuring the tremendous waste of human and material resources which resulted from this policy of 'progress at any price'. Millions of roubles' worth of precious equipment was squandered as a result of faulty planning decisions, often taken under political pressure.

A simultaneous drive to eliminate private farming and to substitute unpopular collective farms led to a famine which cost at least 5 million lives. Peasants frequently slaughtered their horses or livestock rather than surrender them to the authorities. Those who resisted collectivisation, and even those thought likely to do so, were unceremoniously packed off to forced-labour camps in remote areas, where conditions were atrocious and few survived.

The licensed brutalities of Stalin's 'revolution from above' beggar description. The wounds it inflicted endure to this day. They help to account for the sorry state of Soviet farming, still the weakest sector of the economy. Even after 1933 the Government deliberately continued to give a high priority to investment in industry, particularly heavy industry, at the expense of agriculture. The collective farmers were subjected to strict controls which made them hand over almost their entire crop to the State for a derisory return. They had scarcely any incentive to produce. When the Germans invaded, the collective-farm system collapsed almost overnight. Many peasants demonstrated openly their hostility to the Soviet régime, although they soon found the Nazis even harsher taskmasters.

After the war Stalin was naturally more suspicious of the peasants than ever. The collective-farm system was restored and stiffened by such measures as the merger of several communities to form a single giant agricultural enterprise. Not until Stalin died was the Party's policy to some extent relaxed. Crop prices were raised and compulsory delivery quotas abolished, and farms allowed to purchase tractors and other equipment from the Government.

Khrushchev in particular was anxious to increase food output. But he preferred to concentrate on such expedients as growing maize or ploughing up remote 'virgin lands' instead of granting the peasants the material incentives and independence essential to solve the problem. Before 1914 Russia was the bread-basket of Europe. Today she is obliged to spend precious dollars on importing grain from the New World. The chief difficulty is not technical but ideological: the Party's fear of making concessions that would encourage the peasants' instinctive feeling for private property, a relic of *bourgeois* individualism that has no place in a Socialist society.

The same doctrinaire motive hinders the Party from giving the consumer what he wants. Although industrial output has grown rapidly,* living standards have increased comparatively modestly from their 1928 levels. Such commodities as motor-

* The average annual increase of civilian industrial production for the period 1928–55 has been computed by one Western specialist at 6·9 per cent, or 5·8 per cent taking population changes into account. The rate of growth has declined somewhat in recent years. The annual increase in the gross national product has been estimated at 7 per cent during the years 1950–58 and at 5·5 per cent in 1958–63.

cars, refrigerators or even good-quality clothing and footwear are in short supply, and very costly even when available. The lack of urban housing is critical. While these shortcomings are partly due to the continuing requirements of the producer-goods industries, especially those concerned with defence, they are also partly ideological in origin.

There has long been an implicit assumption among the planners that in a Socialist society they alone should decide what, and how much, the individual might be permitted to consume. Only in recent years has this attitude begun to change. Partly under the example of the other Eastern European countries, the system of planning and industrial management is being decentralised, so that the man on the spot, rather than some distant official, may decide the range and price of goods produced, after estimating the potential demand. A modest element of free enterprise is being introduced into the controlled economy. The average Russian citizen today, especially in the towns, enjoys higher living standards than his grandfather did before the Revolution. But in comparison with other industrialised countries in the West, and even with some in Eastern Europe, the situation still leaves much to be desired. As contacts with the outside world multiply, the man in the street is likely to become increasingly aware of the material opportunities that he is missing. In the Soviet Union, as elsewhere, *l'appétit vient en mangeant*: satisfaction of one demand stimulates an awareness of others. Consumers can be expected to make their wants known indirectly to those in authority.

But it would be naive to assume, as is sometimes done, that this pressure will of itself force the Communist régime to change its nature. The Soviet leaders have themselves often denied that this will happen. They are aware of the problem and will seek to avert it by tapping other sources of loyalty to the system, such as patriotic pride in Soviet cultural and technological achievements. It must not be forgotten that, for all the changes that have occurred in recent years, Soviet society still remains totalitarian.

Perhaps the strongest conviction among the Bolsheviks in 1917 was that the Revolution would put an end to exploitation by introducing an egalitarian classless society. This was seen as the main advantage of Socialism over capitalism. The desire for social levelling was particularly marked in the early years of the régime. The old 'ruling classes' were dispossessed and external marks of status abolished. But even then exceptions had to be made in favour of '*bourgeois* specialists' whose services were required to fill key jobs in the armed forces or the economy. In the 1920s much was done to build up a new 'technical intelligentsia', mainly (but not entirely) recruited from the working classes, whose members would be politically loyal and capable of supervising and eventually supplanting these specialists.

To this end education was promoted on a massive scale. A special campaign was waged to eliminate illiteracy By 1940 the number of pupils in primary and secondary schools had more than trebled, and those receiving higher education quadrupled, as compared with 1914. The industrialisation drive greatly augmented the need for skilled managers in every field, and Stalin adjusted Bolshevik doctrine accordingly. Egalitarianism was denounced as a reactionary idea which 'has nothing in common with Marxism-Leninism'. In the mid-1930s, after the heroic endeavours of the First Five-year Plan, Soviet society was officially declared to be Socialist. Class antagonism had allegedly been abolished; the USSR was said to have only two 'friendly' classes—workers and peasants—and an intermediate stratum, the 'toiling intelligentsia', which served their interests.

This formula is still current today, when Soviet society is supposedly in the phase of 'completion of Socialist construction and transition to Communism', the 'main bases' of which are to be laid by 1980. When full Communism is reached, all differences between workers by hand and brain or in town and country are to be overcome, the State will wither away, and income will be related to social need rather than the amount of work done.

Actually, the present social pattern is more complex than

Soviet theorists admit, and there are considerable differences of income, prestige and power. Whether the USSR deserves to be called Socialist is really a semantic question, the answer to which depends on one's views of what Marx meant by the term. There is certainly a good deal of social mobility by comparison with Tsarist Russia or even some capitalist countries today. But it is less easy for children of workers and peasants, especially the latter, to rise into the élite than official spokesmen claim. Members of this élite enjoy high salaries, supplemented by bonuses and other awards; in their way of life and social attitudes they often differ radically from their fellow-citizens employed in manual labour.

But these privileges are conditional and do not confer established rights. Monetary income cannot easily be translated into property; there is of course no stock market in which individuals can invest; and inheritance laws are strict. Extensive private accumulation of wealth is officially frowned upon as a sign of un-Socialist tendencies. The Soviet 'ruling class' is essentially a political, not a social, élite. Its members exercise power only within the limits permitted by the Party. Since Soviet society offers little scope for autonomous pressures, it is wishful thinking to believe that current trends are bringing it closer to the Western pattern, until the two will ultimately converge. It is more likely that, provided the régime survives, its leaders will succeed in bringing about Communism—not as Marx envisaged it, but as it is now defined in the USSR.

The official image of the future, as presented in the 1961 Party programme, looks less like a fulfilment of the original Marxist prophecy than a picture of present-day Russia, with many of its existing blemishes perpetuated. Although the State is to wither away under full Communism, the Party is to survive—and to continue to perform its guiding role in society. It is the Party, for instance, which will decide how much the individual citizen 'needs' and receives from common funds. Expressed in this form, Communism is not an impracticable utopia. Whether it is still a desirable goal, worth such a tremendous effort to achieve, is another question.

It is in the political field, more than any other, that the gulf is greatest between the original hopes of the Revolution and actual achievement. To the men of 1917 Socialism meant the transfer of effective power to the toiling masses. Alas, the logic of events soon turned their 'dictatorship of the proletariat' into a dictatorship of the Party, or more correctly of the Party leaders or leader. Already Lenin, as we have seen, disregarded democratic forms where they threatened to impair administrative efficiency, and Stalin established his personal ascendancy in an even more obvious form. By 1928 he had eliminated Trotsky and other potential rivals in a bitter struggle for the succession to Lenin. By manipulating a pliant 'apparatus' of officials who owed their positions to his patronage, he was able to control opinion within the ruling Communist Party.

Other parties had long since vanished from the scene. During the NEP period it was still possible for political dissent to be expressed indirectly in literary or scholarly works. But the 'Stalin revolution' destroyed even this limited freedom. All cultural activities were brought under strict Party control. Writers, artists and scientists became servants of the régime, whose duty it was to extol the glories of 'Socialist construction' and the infallible genius of Stalin. In consequence public life virtually atrophied.

The Party became a kind of bureaucratic extension of the dictator's own personality. Its congresses were turned into demonstrative rallies of the faithful. In the late 1930s Stalin and his supporters resorted to mass terror against their real or supposed enemies. Countless Soviet citizens, Communists as well as non-Communists, disappeared without trace in a series of 'purges', which had no rational justification other than that they made the omnipotent dictator feel less insecure. Stalin feared the Old Bolsheviks who had made the Revolution as an embarrassing reminder of a past he was anxious to forget, or to remould according to his own fancy. Their removal from office opened the way for a new generation of men who had been schooled in the harsh struggles of the 1930s and were utterly devoted to their Leader. Even so,

Stalin distrusted them. He was preparing yet another bloody purge when death overtook him in March, 1953.

His successors, among whom Nikita Khrushchev soon rose to pre-eminence, were themselves cast in the Stalinist mould, and therefore found it difficult to dissociate themselves entirely from his legacy. In February, 1956, Khrushchev delivered his sensational 'secret speech', in which he exposed some (but not all) of the crimes of the Stalin era. By suddenly shattering the myth of the late dictator's infallibility he cast doubts upon the legitimacy of his own régime. Ordinary citizens again began to think about political issues that had long been taboo. An intellectual ferment got under way which the Party tried hard to keep under control, especially when the Hungarian Revolution in October, 1956, provided a graphic object lesson as to what might happen if the opposition were to get out of hand. Khrushchev claimed that the 'cult of personality' under Stalin had been just an incidental blemish upon an otherwise healthy organism; an individual leader might err, but the Party as such could not; and with himself at the helm it was steering the correct course toward the bright Communist future.

A number of measures, or half-measures, were taken which somewhat improved the political climate in the USSR. The secret police were brought under stricter Party control, but were still allowed a good deal of power over ordinary citizens. A new criminal code (1958) laid down that a man could only be punished for an actual offence; it did not, however, give an accused person the right to a free trial in open court, or do away with the many other legal abuses that had enabled the Stalinists to commit their massive crimes. Congresses of the Party were called regularly, and the rank-and-file members encouraged to show more initiative in carrying out its policies; but important decisions continued to be taken at the top. Similar efforts were made to reinvigorate the soviets and trade unions, which had been reduced by Stalin to passive instruments of the Party's will. All these were gestures rather than real steps in the direction of liberty and democracy. But it was a measure of Russia's political progress under Khrushchev that in October, 1964, he could be removed from power comparatively painlessly, without any violence being done to him or a major purge of his supporters taking place.

Fifty years after the Revolution Russia is as far away as ever from the rule of law or popular control of the Government. But it can at least be said that she is enjoying a precarious political stability under a dictatorship which, although it rests ultimately upon force, commands a fair amount of public assent.

It is unlikely that any future Communist leader will find it necessary to resort to the brutal terroristic methods of Stalin. Viewed in broad perspective, the extreme form of totalitarian rule which he introduced, and maintained for a quarter-century, was a concomitant of rapid industrialisation. Having once decided on a crash programme to change the face of Russia, tyranny became inevitable. The population had to be compelled to submit, to accept present sacrifices for the sake of future gains. The prospect of 'jam tomorrow', when tomorrow never comes, is not one that people are likely to accept voluntarily.

This does not mean that all Stalin's excesses were 'necessary' and therefore justifiable. Many of them were simply the product of his own paranoiac fears. Nor does it follow that Russia had no alternative but to advance at such a breakneck pace: a more balanced use of human and material resources would undoubtedly have brought more satisfactory results. Unfortunately it is in the nature of Communism to encourage extreme solutions of this kind.

Much the same verdict may be passed upon the whole Soviet experience during the last half-century. Viewed historically, Communism has been a means of reconciling the Russian people to the hardships inseparable from the process of modernising a backward country. It has not brought nearer the principal objectives for which it ostensibly stands: international peace and brotherhood, economic and social justice, freedom and democracy for the labouring masses. But the myth that it *is* accomplishing these goals performs a useful social function, in winning the loyalty of millions of people and harnessing their abundant energies to the task of social reconstruction.

Yet to many people the price that it has exacted may seem too high. Other countries have achieved progress with less sacrifice of human life, less infraction of basic rights and freedoms, less disturbance of the international order—and finally, with less arrogance by their leaders. The Soviet Communists have boasted for fifty years that their experience, and theirs alone, provides a valid model for the rest of mankind to follow. But this extravagant claim is belied by the record, of which people outside and inside the USSR are becoming increasingly aware. The Communist achievement, impressive as it is in many ways, is less so when seen in international perspective.

Moreover, it appears that Communism may now be on the verge of fulfilling its historic mission in Russia and so rendering itself superfluous. As the Soviet economy enters upon the stage of industrial maturity, it ceases to stand in such need of a political authority capable of suppressing undesirable consumer demand and enforcing modern labour discipline upon recalcitrant peasants. On the contrary, ideologically-inspired interference in planning and administrative decisions which must by nature be highly technical can do more harm than good. It makes it difficult, if not impossible, to arrive at rational solutions of complex problems.

Similarly, a society that is becoming increasingly well-educated and sophisticated cannot but find the crude tenets of Marxism-Leninism lacking in credibility. Members of the younger generation in particular resent the many restrictions on individual liberty, the puritanical moral code, and the hypocrisy prevalent in so many areas of Soviet public life. Half-consciously, they are seeking to re-assert their validity as individuals, and to discover for themselves what is true and what is false in the world about them.

Intellectuals, especially writers, can sometimes give expression to this basic human striving. 'When I hear people speak of re-shaping life,' says a character in Boris Pasternak's *Dr Zhivago*, 'it makes me lose my self-control. . . . People who can say that have never understood a thing about life. . . . They look upon it as a lump of raw material which needs to be processed by them, to be ennobled by their touch. But life is never a material, a substance to be moulded. If you want to know, life is the principle of self-renewal, it is constantly renewing and re-making and changing and transfiguring itself, it is infinitely beyond your or my theories about it.'

In their search for alternative solutions to Russia's problems these new questing spirits naturally look towards the West, whose values appeal all the more because they are, so to speak, forbidden fruit. Such contacts are discouraged in many ways by officialdom, but they are no longer prohibited altogether. In these circumstances the Western nations bear a heavy responsibility to live up as best they can to their own ideals—to their democratic and liberal principles, rooted as they are in the Christian humanist tradition. It should be recognised that young Russians of the 1960s do not approach the West in the spirit of uncritical adulation that their forefathers did before the Revolution. The past half-century has given them a rich experience on which to base their judgment, and they have a keen eye for our frailties. It would be a tragedy if these men, having lived through totalitarian rule and rejected it as incompatible with the natural dignity of man, should find the Western mode of life archaic, decadent or irrelevant to their needs.

Bibliography

R. P. Browder & A. F. Kerensky, *The Russian Provisional Government 1917: Documents and Materials*. Hoover Institution, Stanford, Calif., 1961. Three volumes.
A valuable collection of sources on the period March–November, 1917.

J. Bunyan and H. H. Fisher, *The Bolshevik Revolution, 1917–8. Documents and Materials*. Hoover War Library, Stanford, Calif., 1934. Reprinted 1965.
A detailed collection of sources on the period October, 1917–April, 1918.

W. H. Chamberlin, *The Russian Revolution, 1917–1921*. Two volumes. 1935. Paperback edition: Universal Library, Grosset & Dunlap, N.Y., 1965.
The best general history of the Revolution and its aftermath by an American journalist.

R. Charques, *The Twilight of Imperial Russia*. 1959. Paperback edition: Oxford U.P., 1965.
A sympathetic account by a British scholar of the reign of Nicholas II.

I. Deutscher, *Stalin: a Political Biography*. 1949. O.U.P. Paperback edition, 1961.
A masterly biography of the Soviet leader.

I. Deutscher, *Trotsky: the Prophet Armed, 1879–1921*. O.U.P., 1954. Paperback edition: Vintage Books, Knopf & Random House, N.Y., 1965.
The first volume of a three-volume work on Lenin's right-hand man in the Revolution.

M. Fainsod, *How Russia is Ruled*. 2nd edition. Harvard–Oxford U.P., 1963.
An expert survey of the Soviet political system by an American scholar.

M. T. Florinsky, *Russia: a History and an Interpretation*. Vol. 2. Collier–Macmillan, 1953. Reprinted 1963.

The best general history of Russia in English. This volume covers the period 1801–1920.

A. F. Kerensky, *The Kerensky Memoirs: Russia and History's Turning Point*. Cassell, 1966.

The autobiography of the Prime Minister of Russia from July to November, 1917.

R. Pipes, *The Formation of the Soviet Union: Communism and Nationalism, 1917–1923*. Harvard–Oxford U.P., 1954. Revised edition, 1964.

An analysis of the Bolsheviks' handling of the national minorities in Russia during and after the Revolution.

O. H. Radkey, *The Agrarian Foes of Bolshevism: Promise and Default of the Socialist-Revolutionaries, March–October 1917*. Columbia U.P., New York, 1958.

A critical analysis of the Bolsheviks' principal rivals for power during the Revolutionary period; the first of two volumes on the subject.

J. Reed, *Ten Days that Shook the World*. 1926. Paperback edition: Penguin Books, Harmondsworth, 1966.

A classic account of the Bolshevik Revolution by an American journalist strongly sympathetic to the Bolsheviks.

L. B. Schapiro, *The Origin of the Communist Autocracy*. Bell, 1955. Paperback edition: Praeger, N.Y., 1965.

A study of the Bolsheviks' treatment of their political opponents during the Revolutionary period.

L. B. Schapiro, *The Communist Party of the Soviet Union*. 1960. Paperback edition: Methuen, 1964.

A critical history of the Communist Party from its origins to the present.

H. Seton-Watson, *The Decline of Imperial Russia, 1855–1914*. 1953. 2nd edition, Methuen, 1964.

D. Shub, *Lenin: a Biography*. Pelican Original: Penguin Books, Harmondsworth, 1966.

The best single-volume biography of the founder of world Communism.

L. Trotsky, *History of the Russian Revolution*. 1932–3. Abridged edition by F. W. Dupee. Doubleday, Garden City, N.Y., 1959.
A lively but partisan picture of the Revolution by one of its leading participants.

B. D. Wolfe, *Three Who Made a Revolution*. 1948. Revised paperback edition: Dell, N. Y., 1964.
Biographies of Lenin, Trotsky and Stalin to 1914.